Praise for *Get Me C*

"Jeremy shares his thoughts and feelings in an extremely candid, uncompromising style."
—Denny Zeitlin, jazz pianist and composer

"Jeremy was the most complete artist and the most relentlessly creative individual I have ever met. . . . He breathed art and music twenty-four hours a day. Steig's notes are as clear and soaring as ever in this chronicle of Greenwich Village in the '60s and the music and art scene that he was so much a part of and helped create."
—Andrew Smith, former Head Writer, *Saturday Night Live*

"Great story and great book! It takes you on a whirlwind tour of music of the '60s and the '70s.
—Bruce Spiegel, film director of *Bill Evans: Time Remembered*

"Jeremy was the most original jazz flutist of his era, and his memoir is a fascinating and often jarring glimpse into the realities of the hardscrabble jazz life. Fasten your seatbelts, you're in for a bumpy ride. A must read."
—Ron Micci, flutist, Paige Brook student, and author of *Addie & Me*

"Jeremy was a breath of fresh air. He was kind and loved irony and the idiosyncrasies of life in general. He also played his ass off."
—Racey Gilbert, jazz drummer, photographer, and entrepreneur

"I've known Jeremy for decades and had no idea what a truly fascinating life he had. I'm blown away by this interesting and entertaining memoir."
—Glenn Franke, leader of the Glenn Franke Big Band

"Jeremy has left us his thoughts in a trenchant, incisive, sardonic last testament, peppered with his ingenious sketches. . . . This is an absorbing self-portrait of a multifaceted artist."
—Karla Munger, childhood friend

"I'm so grateful to have had the opportunity to read this memoir and learn more about the creative journey of his life path. . . . Jeremy is a teacher for those of us who have struggled with our own creativity in our life."
—Ellen Olian Bate, retired attorney and alumnus of Music & Art High School

"Jeremy Steig is possibly the most interesting and talented jazz flute player ever. *Get Me Out of Here* is a peek into how he got there. It gives clear and personal insight into what growing up in the New York jazz scene from the late 1950s on was like for him. It is a wonderfully articulate and delightful tale about a very complex artist, his dysfunctional family, and his friends and lovers."
—Stuart Bigley, cofounder and former Executive Director, Unison Arts Center

GET ME OUT
OF HERE

GET ME OUT OF HERE

JEREMY STEIG

BYROAD PRESS

Byroad Press
www.byroadpress.com

ORDERING INFORMATION

Quantity sales. Special discounts are available on quantity purchases by corporations, associations, and others. For details, contact publisher@byroadpress.com.

Orders by US trade bookstores and wholesalers. Please contact BCH: (800) 431-1579 or visit www.bookch.com for details.

ISBN: 978-4-9911279-1-5 (pkb)
       978-4-9911279-2-2 (ebook)

Printed in the United States.

First Edition

25 24 23 22 21 20   10 9 8 7 6 5 4 3 2

Book producer and text designer: Marin Bookworks

Editor: PeopleSpeak

In memory of Frac

CONTENTS

FOREWORD

For the first four years of my life, our family lived on Perry Street in Greenwich Village; it was a multifloor brownstone that my father bought in 1928. Directly behind our house the backyard became the backyard for a building on Charles Street. In that building was the apartment that Jeremy lived in with his mother, Liza, and his sister Lucy. Liza's better-known sister and Jeremy's aunt—Margaret Mead—lived in our basement apartment, along with her daughter (and Jeremy's cousin), Mary Catherine Bateson. Liza was my mother's closest friend—they were both left-handed, intuitive, and quirky; and they had lots of laughs together. Lucy Steig was sometimes my babysitter. My older brother was, for a time, Jeremy's roommate in that Charles Street apartment, after our family, and Liza, moved to Boston. Liza and my mother stayed close—Liza was a frequent dinner guest at our home in suburban Boston.

Liza provided me with a chance to have a second mother, one more radical than my own. She watched out for me, and she was a great person to talk things over with. We traveled in England together a couple of times. I spent a lot of time in Liza's art studio at Lesley College, where we would paint or do ceramics or make papier mâché.

Jeremy came up to Boston to play gigs and sometimes stay at Liza's Cambridge apartment.

Jeremy's first album, *Flute Fever*, was straight jazz but so energized with his signature sound. Then came the Satyrs, which was something totally new. In the late '60s, my friends and I would be first in line sitting on the sidewalk outside Club 47 in Cambridge so as to get in to see Jeremy and the Satyrs. Over the years, we went to hear Jeremy at the Jazz Workshop in Boston and other Boston gigs.

A friend and I would travel to New York City to visit Jeremy in the Charles Street apartment. It was an interesting environment—we could sit in his father's Reichian orgone box. At that point, Jeremy's murals covered most of the walls. It was easy to hang out and listen to jazz and meet the occasional colleagues who dropped by. Jeremy directed me to check out new sounds he thought were worthwhile, such as when he advised me to see the Mothers of Invention when they were playing at the Garrick in the Village. I was grateful that Jeremy took me under his wing during my teenage years and that he was willing to be a friend and talk candidly about whatever was on his mind. He offered choice observations about the world and the family, nothing held back.

There were many years we didn't see each other. In 1989, my brother's death prompted me to call. Jeremy recorded and mailed me a tape of improvised solo flute to play at my brother's memorial in New Hampshire.

In 2009, I made a visit to New York and arranged to see Jeremy and Asako. I didn't realize that it would be my last time to see him in person. It was just before he moved to Japan. Asako and Jeremy had made his current apartment into a digital recording studio and had produced *Pterodactyl*, among other things. During the visit he shared an early version of this autobiography. He told me the manuscript was something for Asako to publish after he was gone.

He was ready to get out of New York City and the United States. His life in the New York City environment was stressful; the Village wasn't the same place as when we were young. The music industry had become tough for musicians like Jeremy. He was someone for whom improvisational collaboration and whole-body music expression wasn't just a gig but a style of consciousness. His consciousness was, at that point, looking for a safe harbor.

After I got home, I read the bio. Here suddenly were the backstories of the family I knew, but there was a lot I didn't know at all—his complex family and complex life was open to view; it was, for me, riveting. It was a story that reveals Jeremy as a keen observer—an unjudgmental observer, staying curious, someone who had experienced life's events in an almost childlike state of wonder, watching and taking note of the fascinating behaviors around him. It was as though his Aunt Margaret's anthropological eyes had found their way into Jeremy's vision as well. And I got it why he wanted it published posthumously.

More recently, rereading Jeremy's life story, this colorful collection of characters that populated his life, and after discussing it with Asako, a theme for this story has emerged: the place—Greenwich Village in the '40s, '50s, '60s, and beyond; the family of origin—Liza, a spontaneous bohemian mom for whom art opportunities popped to life in each moment, Bill Steig whose life was a prodigious stream of cartoons, books, and unconventional explorations, and Lucy, a prolific and naturally brilliant painter; and Jeremy's fundamental nature as a feeling type/observer/jazz flute prodigy—it all led to a near inevitable circumstance. Jeremy was shaped by a confluence of potent influences. As a result, one concludes that his allegiance to a high standard for creative expression is second nature. He wasn't well equipped to be strategic or ambitious in the arc of his career. The standard for artistic integrity was set high, a standard he took quite seriously and one that didn't make things easy for him. Scripted art forms, cynical music producers, and opportunistic musicians, he appears to experience all these with some measure of amazement and appropriate irony. Perhaps, there's a "What I am doing here?" embedded within the "Get me out of here" title to the story. Eventually, fortunately, he had a chance to step into a new chapter of life with Asako when he moved to Japan, a place that made sense to him, a place where, in my experience, artistic refinement and gentle respect for creativity is woven into seemingly every facet of life.

For Jeremy, the life of a jazz artist was, in part, a felt responsibility to stay fresh and alive to the unknown, to find something new to discover in each performance and with every collaboration. It's a blessing, of course, to be cast in this role but also kind of a burden to be sworn to such a pure creative path. And it's a path that leaves one recursively vulnerable to people who sense opportunity for predation and imitation. It's a path that can involve disappointment that requires asking, "Huh, what just happened?"

The narrative that Jeremy recounts, in a voice distinctly formed from the richness of his background, about the tunes he played and the visual creations he painted and drew, with its dry wit, is an earnest commentary. What kind of commentary? Would it be fair to call it a rant (like Job's rant to God)? Not at all. That's not Jeremy's style or preoccupation. Or resigned afterword that invites the reader to share with him and protest the sad state of "true jazz," at least in his experience of it? That's too sentimental and bitter for this person. Maybe we could call it a tender "for what it's worth." Jeremy, unshackled from any remaining unrealistic expectations, came to accept that an artful life has bits of glory but maybe also much that is bittersweet—and along with that note, a sobering acknowledgment of the tentative condition of our species.

That a friend, who had never set out to be a writer, took the time and effort to delicately and carefully recount this unusual life story, one that spells out considerable vulnerability incurred staying present and adaptable to crazy twists and turns, feels like a kindness. Readers may find recognition inside themselves, upon reflection, of the raw poetry of the life and death that happens in each moment—the opening to the realization that in this present moment alone is the place of wonder and creativity. And we may notice how this sense of wonder or newness contrasts to the way art can become, to one degree or another, deadened when it involves grasping for recognition and accomplishment. I hear Jeremy offering a gentle invitation to notice the choices we make for how we meet the challenge of art (and life) and the possibility to examine what creativity is fundamentally about. Reading his words offers us an opportunity to listen to Jeremy's music knowing something about the heart from whom it springs.

Kevin Frank
Coauthor of *How Life Moves*
Holderness, New Hampshire
June 1, 2019

ACKNOWLEDGMENTS

Many thanks to Alan, Bert, Joel, Jonathan, Kevin, Mayapriya, Peter, and Sharon.

If Jeremy were here, he would say, "Solid!"

Asako

NOTE TO THE READER

On September 6, 2003, Jeremy asked me, out of the blue, how to write on the computer. I showed him the basic features of a word processing program, and he began to write. He seemed really into it. He crouched over the keyboard and kept typing with his index fingers. Every thirty seconds or so, he looked up at the monitor to go over what he had just entered. He sometimes giggled as he typed.

The outcome of his initial writing spell, which lasted for about a month and a half, was a collection of anecdotes with single-word titles. He also did illustrations for some of the anecdotes. I read them and said that I really liked them. He said, "I'm doing this as a therapy."

On March 27, 2016, twelve and a half years later, Jeremy and I found ourselves in a hospital room in Yokohama, Japan. He sat up on the bed and read aloud to me the lastest addition to the manuscript he had just handwritten. He then asked me to close it by putting down my view of our life together and somehow publish it.

What you are about to read is the result of our intermittent spells at the computer keyboard that took place over sixteen years in total.

Please note that inserting a gallery of Jeremy's drawings was entirely my idea. He was a prolific artist, and the selection in this book is only a fragmental representation of his works.

Asako
September 2019

Part I

JEREMY'S STORY

One

STRANGE ROOTS

*When my father, William (Bill) Steig, was a kid he was playing on a
frozen pond. The ice gave way and he went under. That would have
been the end of him, and me, too, but a man reached in and pulled
him out just in the nick of time.*

was born in 1942 in New York City. When I was three, America
dropped atom bombs on Hiroshima and Nagasaki, and my father
left my mother. He moved about eight blocks away to West
Twelfth Street. I was allowed to see him once a week, but strangely
enough, these weekly visits became the most vivid memories of my
early childhood.

Having discovered free love through his guru, Wilhelm Reich
(more about him later), my father would change girlfriends every few
months. On my visits, my father, his girlfriend, and I would all sleep

in the same bed. One morning, I started climbing over the naked body of a girlfriend of his. My father said to me, "Don't you think she's a little big for you?" to which I replied, "No dame's too big for me."

I don't know how that language got into my head, but that's what I said. Women were my first interest.

I lived with my mother, Liza, and my older sister, Lucy, at 63 Charles Street in Greenwich Village. We had a whole floor of the building at a very cheap rent. My first memory of the apartment was waking up every morning to a beautiful painting that Stuart Davis had given to my father. I once made a small hole in it with my toy bow and arrow, and my grandfather patched it up. Several years later, my father took the painting back from my mother and sold it for

$2,000 so he could give the money to the Wilhelm Reich Defense Fund. About ten years ago, I saw the same painting hanging in the Metropolitan Museum.

I had a windup record player. Each needle was good for one play of a 78rpm record. My father left his record collection behind in his haste to get away from Liza. It was a very nice collection. Some of my favorite artists were Lead Belly, Albert Ammons, James P. Johnson, Sidney Bechet, Bessie Smith, Benny Goodman ("Muskrat Ramble"), Louis Armstrong ("I'll Be Glad When You're Dead, You Rascal, You"), and John Jacob Niles. I also had three race records of Robert Johnson. My father's record collection gave me a good introduction to music.

My father sent me to camp every summer for two months and paid for private school. All other expenses fell on my mother, so she went to work. Her first job was painting flowers on plates. She got $10 a day. When the union went on strike, she got $25 for picketing. She cracked up when she found out that she had been marching for a communist union.

We didn't have much money, and Liza sometimes had to improvise. For instance, she used orange crates as our bookcases. My classmates at school were by and large very wealthy. Many of them lived in townhouses and had maids, while I spent a good part of my time playing in the street unsupervised. In those days, parents weren't paranoid about their children being kidnapped. I got a good view of both ends of society.

When I was six, I started playing the recorder and discovered the magic of music. Leanor Scoville was my recorder teacher. She was the first person who got me excited about playing music. I understood how to read music from the first day. She had hundreds of music books, including a complete wall of Bach scores. It was a fabulous collection. In addition to my lessons with Leanor, I experimented on my own. I found that I could play melodies off the radio by ear.

And soon I was making up counterpoint parts. Years passed before I realized I had the jazz gene. The jazz gene gives you the ability to improvise music with a sense of swing. No scientist has found it yet, but my gut feeling tells me that it's there.

I took lessons with Leanor for about two years until she was evicted from her apartment on Cornelia Street for having too many books. The landlord said that the floor was sinking because of their weight. The story was in the news for a few days. Newspapers called her the book lady as if it was weird to own a lot of beautiful books filled with vital musical information. Leanor had to move and ended up living in a railroad flat next to the train tracks.

In the two years I studied with her, I came to realize that most grownups had no understanding of music. I remember an incident in a candy store. The owner was a nasty guy and he felt like picking on me. First he told me I was a spoiled kid. Then he called me fresh. I replied, "How can I be fresh and spoiled at the same time?" Then I said, "Can you play the recorder?" When he said, "No," I said, "Well, I can."

Being able to play a musical instrument gave me power. I needed it because I was terrible in school. However, this power didn't amount to anything with other kids, who were impressed only if you could hit a baseball over the fence.

Liza's next job was teaching art at a girls' school in Harlem. This took all her energy, and she'd come home exhausted, lie down, and read detective stories. So I ended up spending a lot of time with the Kilb brothers. They lived around the corner from me on Bleecker Street with their parents, Herman the German and Aglaia, who was Greek. Paul Kilb was two years older than I, and Johnny, two years younger. We could reach each other's apartment by going over the roofs and up and down the fire escapes. Since Liza wasn't much of a cook, I often ate dinner with the Kilbs. Herman wouldn't let me in his house unless I said, "Hi, Pop." It made me angry because he wasn't my father. I didn't realize until recently that I was shipped off to another family when my father shipped himself out.

One day, I was playing with the Kilb brothers and Herman came back from outside very excited. He had a copy of the *Daily News* in his hands. In big bold letters was an announcement that the United States had successfully tested the first hydrogen bomb.

"This is wonderful news," he said.

At that moment, I began to wonder if adults were as smart as they claimed to be.

Herman was a carpenter and had built a small boat with a motor in the back. One day, he took Johnny and me to City Island. Johnny and I dropped Herman off on a small island of rocks with a fifth of Imperial whiskey and went fishing. When we came back to pick him up, the bottle was empty. Herman then drove us back to the Village without incident. In those days, most of the adults I came in contact with were alcoholics. My mother was no exception. She was a favorite at drinking parties because she got very funny when soused. I was in the habit of staying up later than I should and witnessed adults behaving badly at my house.

On weekends, Liza painted with a cigarette in one hand or a drink in the other. She sometimes would paint on four or five canvases at a time. While the oil paint was drying on one, she would work on another. She taught me about creativity by example. A flower child before the expression was coined, she dressed in her own way, wearing capes and wide-brimmed hats. One of my father's few fond memories of Liza was her decorating her hair with kumquats ("baby oranges" in my father's words). When she played the piano everything was made up. She had her own style of speech, which was something akin to the bebop language of jazz musicians. For example, Massachusetts became "Massa-two-shits."

I lived in two different worlds: my mother's world and the rest of the world. She and I understood each other perfectly, but I sometimes couldn't make the transition to the outside world. My sister Lucy was my opposite. She didn't know what the hell her mother was talking about. This created big problems for them, and they fought almost every day. Lucy would scream at Liza, and Liza would come back with a song:

Nobody likes me
Everybody hates me
I'm going out in the garden
And eat worms

When Liza got angry, she might say, "Why don't you dry up and blow away?" and raised her upper lip. My mother was just too creative for her own good. It was her style. I wasn't going to try to be like her, so why let it bother me?

Despite all her eccentricities, Liza worked very hard to take care of us. She was a dedicated teacher—perhaps too dedicated. One day, she took her class at the girls' school on a sketching trip in the park. The students attacked her and beat her up badly. It was very upsetting to see her come home all black and blue. She told me that she had tried to break up a fight between two students, and the whole class attacked her. After that, she went back to school to get her master's degree so she could teach at a college.

I had a strange, small part in her getting her degree. One evening, when walking down Fourth Street, I heard the taunt "Faggot." I was being challenged. I replied, "Fuck you," and ended up wrestling in the gutter with this kid, whose name was Walsh. Unfortunately, his friend came over and stabbed me in the back with a knife. Someone yelled that the cops were coming, and we all ran. When I got home and took off my coat, my back was covered with blood. Liza had to take me to the hospital. She was already late with a construction that she had to submit for her class and used my having been stabbed as an excuse to get an extension on her homework.

The only piece of advice she insisted on me learning from her was that I should never get anyone pregnant. She actually sent a couple of my girlfriends to a gynecologist to be fitted for diaphragms. She told me that on a few occasions she helped some women get safe abortions from a doctor in Pennsylvania whom she knew about. Abortions were illegal at that time.

By now, you must be wondering what kind of family Liza came from. She belonged to the Mead family. Everyone in the family was highly educated except for my mother, who did finally get her master's. The family is best known for Liza's older sister, Margaret, the anthropologist.

I have little memory of Grandpa Mead, who taught finance at the University of Pennsylvania. He was always talking politics at the dinner table and did not recognize the children's presence. According to my father, Grandpa Mead always missed the toilet bowl when he took a leak because he was afraid to look at his own dick. My grandmother was in the women's suffrage movement. By the time I was introduced to her, she was very old and did not speak at all. Sitting in her chair, she looked like *Whistler's Mother*.

Aunt Margaret was an interesting type. When I was a child I saw her often. She lived a block away on Perry Street. When she phoned, she never said hello or good-bye. I would hear her say "Jemmy" (my nickname) in a deep froglike voice, say what she was going to say, and click. I never liked the way she pushed my mother around, but she wasn't boring. In fact, she was an encyclopedia. She acted as if she was the world's foremost authority. As I grew up, I began to see that the world at large thought of her that way, but when I was little, she was just Aunt Margaret. Liza met my father at a party, during which Margaret had planned to fix her up with his younger brother, Arthur. Instead, my father, who also was at that party, took Liza home.

I remember having a big argument with Margaret when I was eleven or twelve. We were discussing if homosexuality was natural. She would talk about any subject with me. I told her a story about a man who lived on my block. He tried to molest me, and I barely escaped from his apartment. I had a lot of anger because of this. Aunt Margaret argued that if the culture accepted homosexuality, then being gay was okay. It turned out that she was right. It also turned out that she was gay herself. A few years after Margaret had died, her daughter, Cathy, outed her in her autobiography, *With a Daughter's Eye*. Margaret kept her sexual orientation a secret all her life. I guess she didn't think society was ready.

To an eleven-year-old boy, a child molester was the most obvious example of a gay man. Margaret should have pointed out to me the difference between them. Then again, I wonder what she would have thought if child molesting was accepted by society.

My mother had another sister, Priscilla. We all called her Aunt Pam. Her claim to fame was having had a date with Rudy Vallée. Everyone on both sides of my family needed credentials. Pam married the writer Leo Rosten, who was the author of *Captain Newman, M.D.* This book was later made into a movie, starring Tony Curtis. The character was based on Ralph Greenson, who was Marilyn Monroe's analyst at the time of her death.

Every Thanksgiving, the Meads would gather at Aunt Pam's. The adults sat at a huge, round, polished table in the living room. The children had to eat in the kitchen so that the adults could engage in heavy discussion about politics and other things the kids weren't supposedly ready for. Pam was nice but not very interesting. She showed very little emotion. After we went home from the 1959 Thanksgiving dinner, she slit her throat. According to Lucy, Aunt Margaret and her daughter, Cathy, discovered the body. Margaret made Cathy wipe up the blood. No wonder Margaret couldn't remember it in her own autobiography, where she wrote that Pam got sick and died.

After Aunt Pam's funeral, my great aunt Beth, who was the wealthiest member of the family by her marriage to the founder of Whirlpool, took Liza, Lucy, and me to a French restaurant for lunch. They told me it was the most expensive in New York. I had a crêpe. I think it had lobster in it but it tasted terrible and I couldn't eat. For me, funerals have always been appetite depressants. The waiter came over to me and in a thick French accent said, "What's wrong? You don't like your crêpe?"

It sounded like he said "crap." I replied, "It sure was."

I was very close to Joe, my grandfather on my father's side. He lived on Jane Street, which was a short walk away from where I lived. I saw him often and watched my first television show at his apartment. He was a Polish Jew but gave up being Jewish on the day he kicked a rabbi in the ass. When I tried to get more information about this story from my father, he was already ninety. He just laughed and said, "Joe really hated that rabbi."

Joe spent a year in a Polish jail for having tried to form a union about eighty years before Lech Wałęsa, who succeeded and received a Nobel Prize for his efforts. Joe was a house painter. He never threw anything out and made beautiful toys for all the kids in the family with the scraps he saved. He taught me his style of doodling and gave me a great lesson about color. One day, Joe was working on a painting of a painter in the country with an easel and an open paint box. I asked him if I could help, and he said that I could fill in the colors for the tubes of paint. I began to paint each tube with a different color. He stopped me and said, "No, no, no, all you need is a few colors," and showed me how to do it. Joe had big warm hands, and I remember him washing my little hands in the sink. He died when I was ten or eleven.

My father, Bill Steig, the cartoonist, enjoyed putting the Meads down. Bill always said that my mother didn't know what she was talking about and told me not to believe anything she said. He also said that Aunt Margaret was a "shithead." Although I liked Margaret, I thought that she was much too full of herself, and as a child, I enjoyed hearing him say these things. To me, it didn't matter if my parents got along. But when I asked Bill why I couldn't live with him instead of my mother, he said something like "A child should be with his mother" and dropped the subject. Not much of an answer.

My father always presented the Steig family as the creative side of my family. He made cartoons for the *New Yorker* magazine. On my weekly visits, I used to watch how he composed a drawing by looking over his shoulder. He was very logical in the way he put a drawing together and I learned a lot by watching him. He had a way of moving his pen back and forth across the paper—almost like the movement a lie detector makes.

He had three brothers: Irwin, Henry, and Arthur. Irwin was the oldest and worked in advertising. He smoked cigars and talked like Edward G. Robinson. He liked to draw his fingers out of his pockets and say to me "Stick 'em up." He taught me chess when I was six. He was a champion bridge player and wrote two books about playing cards: *Poker for Fun and Profit* and *Play Gin to Win*. Irwin took me to my first baseball game. We share the same birthday, September 23, but we never celebrated together.

Henry was the second oldest. He made shepherd's pipes for fun. He once played alto sax in burlesque shows and wrote a jazz novel called *Send Me Down*. He started a paint business with Uncle Arthur but then left to become a jeweler. The still shot of Marilyn Monroe in *The Seven Year Itch* where her dress gets blown up by the subway draft was taken in front of his shop on Lexington Avenue. You can see the name Henry Steig in the back. He was the only person to get a rear view of that event.

The youngest brother, Arthur, kept making watercolors and inks and became very successful. He named his ink "FW ink." FW was an abbreviation for "Fucking Wonder," an expression that kids used about themselves in those days. You can still buy FW inks at art stores. Arthur liked to draw. Although he invented beautiful colors, he drew only in black and white. Bill used to say, "Arthur makes the best colors. Henry is the best jeweler. My mother is a better painter than Grandma Moses. And of course, I'm the best cartoonist."

Bill was very competitive and way ahead of Muhammed Ali.

He was in therapy with Wilhelm Reich (sometimes referred to as "W. R."). He liked one of Reich's books and looked him up in the phone book and became a patient. W. R. was a therapist who had studied under Sigmund Freud, but his ideas offended a large part of the Western psychological community. W. R. was my dad's guru. Bill did a lot of work for Reich for no pay. Dad illustrated one of his books titled *Listen, Little Man!*, which was an angry tirade against all the people Reich thought had fucked him over. The book is actually very funny, and I recommend it to anyone who is full of anger and needs a release. My father's drawings for it were brilliant. In one of the drawings, a man has a chain attached to his ankle. A dotted line is going through the middle of the chain, breaking it. He looks at the broken chain in horror and says, "Oh, my God."

W. R. thought that the atomic bomb testing screwed up the atmosphere, which damaged people and made them more prone to murder. He also thought that atomic bombs created tornados, earthquakes, hurricanes, and so forth. My father spent two years going through the *Daily News* and the *New York Times* and cutting out all the news concerning murder, domestic violence, weather disturbances, and every atom bomb test for Reich. W. R. also told him to leave my mother. Only a guru has that kind of power over another human being.

Reichian therapy was supposed to make you sexually healthy. That appealed to my father immensely. Bill and Arthur became part of the cult, and their kids were sent to therapy to be "cured." I have seen and heard more than enough to know that Reich was the leader of a cult that abused children. The Catholic Church wasn't set up for the abuse of children but made for a perfect place for chicken hawks to become pederastic priests. The same is true with day care, the Boy Scouts, physical education classes, and the like. In Reichian therapy, you must take your clothes off, and the therapist watches you breathe and does some body work on the patient to get rid of what Reich called "body armor." Once I tried to picture my father and Uncle Arty standing naked in front of the great man, getting poked who knows where. It made me laugh, but I quickly canceled the thought.

A pretty large group of people felt that they had to take their clothes off, get poked, and become "orgasticly potent." It was the beginning of the sexual revolution, and Reich gave everyone license to get laid. If he had stopped there everything would have been fine, but he said, "Bring me your children, and I will make them into soft, loving people."

He made it seem almost like original sin; the children were all considered sick and dragged off to therapy.

Though my mother had already been divorced, she tried to please Bill by sending me to therapy. My older sister, Lucy, and I were sent to Felicia Saxe for treatment.

My cousin Susanna Steig, born in 1944, was also sent to Felicia Saxe and other Reichian therapists. She later wrote an essay about her experiences, which is reproduced below.

"My Childhood Experiences with Reichian Therapy"
By Susanna Steig

I was three years old. What I remember: my mother leading me down the long, dark hallway of our New York City apartment. The cold, tiled hallway. A bus. Going up the stairs of a concrete building, cold, huge and scary (a warehouse, I now realize).

She was sitting in a chair. A gypsy-like woman dressed in shiny silks, with her breasts hanging out of her blouse. Her name was Felicia Saxe. I was left alone with her. The sharp pain of her fingers and nails digging into my shoulders. And then, I was caught up in what felt like a screaming, crying machine that would never stop. My screaming and crying was what she wanted.

More memories: my face coming closer and closer to her breasts, being shoved into her breasts—I couldn't breathe! A huge vagina, coming nearer and nearer to my face. And then, as if from afar, her holding me on her lap, her hand under my skirt, masturbating me.

I remember being on a bus with my mother, on the way there. There were newly blooming spring trees. I said something about what was happening. My mother looked out the window.

When I was an adult my mother told me that she had taken me to this therapy for months and listened to me scream. What was the reason? I was jealous of my younger sister, born when I was two years and two months old, and I was aggressive toward her.

What stopped this was that my father came to pick me up one day, saw what was going on, and decided I was not to go back. He cried and begged my forgiveness. I don't know if my parents noticed that I changed from a happy, boisterous child to a frightened, quiet one.

When I was six, my family moved to rural New Jersey. A year later, my father came to me one day and started telling me everything that was wrong with me. All I remember is that he said I was "too much of a lady," and needed treatment.

My handsome father, my savior, drove me to Red Bank, New Jersey. It was a long ride. We got out and went into a house. We sat, and I heard blood-curdling screams coming from a neighboring room. I was numb. Then, I was led into that room with a big bed, where Ellsworth Baker asked me to take off all my clothes except for my white cotton underwear. And then the pain began— pressing pain, all over my body. He also asked me to lie on my stomach and pressed on my back so hard that I couldn't breathe. This, also, went on for months.

No matter what they did to me, I made no noise, and did not react at all. This was my way of protecting myself. Since this therapy was supposed to provoke a dramatic physical and emotional reaction, I don't know what they thought.

After the first time with Dr. Baker, my father took me to visit a friend. She asked me where I had been, and I was too ashamed to tell her. I said, "PT," meaning physical therapy. I was very ashamed and ate some marshmallows to make me feel better.

That same year, Reich did some experiments at his lab in Rangeley, Maine that apparently turned out to be toxic. I was sent to Maine to keep Peter Reich, Reich's son, company for a week, since we were both seven. We stayed at the home of Myron Sharaf (who later wrote *Fury on Earth*) and his wife Greta. She was pregnant. She later had a son named Peter, who killed himself when he was a teenager, rumored to be because of Greta's affair with Reich.

I loved Peter Reich. He was my friend. We were put to bed together on that first night I was there. Myron and Greta stood over us and said, "Why don't you make love?" Peter and I hugged and kissed. A few minutes later, Myron and Greta came into the room naked. She put in her diaphragm in front of us and said they were going off to make love, also.

One night, Greta showed me some live lobsters in a pot that were to be boiled for our dinner. By the end of the week, I had decided to stop talking.

(Peter Reich later wrote a wonderful book called *A Book of Dreams* about his childhood. He was not a true believer. He was shunned by the Reichian community.)

The treatments with Baker continued when I returned home. He gripped my leg one day and said, "Is this where you feel it when you think of Peter?" I realized that he knew what had happened in Maine and that I was part of an experiment.

Other stories I have heard:

Felicia Saxe was discredited by Reich at some point, after which time a relative of mine, as a child, was sent into treatment with her for years. Despite this, and my father's opinion of her, not one adult in my family lifted a finger to try to save my relative.

Some of the boys who were in treatment with Felicia Saxe, at an older age than I was, were masturbated by her as part of the therapy. Felicia Saxe also ran a summer camp for children, where many horrible experiences happened to relatives of mine. I hope these former children of Reichians tell their stories.

When I was in my fifties, I was visiting my mother, and an old friend of hers was there. I found out for the first time that the friend had sent her younger daughter to therapy with a Reichian who raped her repeatedly for months. The younger daughter was eleven years old at the time. I don't know the name of the therapist, but he was later put into a mental institution.

I wrote to the younger daughter. Her older sister had been my friend when we were children. My friend had been sent to this same therapist when she was five. When she was twenty, she broke with her family and joined a born-again Christian cult. Their mother was distraught because her younger daughter still blamed her for what had happened and insisted that she had known what was going on.

As I said, I hope that all these children of Reichians write their stories. I believe this should be made part of history.

How do I feel now about all this, now that I approach my sixtieth birthday? I have spent a lifetime dealing with the aftermath of my traumatic childhood, full of abuse and betrayal. I am now estranged from most of my family. I am tired of secrets, of people not wanting to know, of a story so outlandish and horrible that I do not really want to inflict it on people unless they really want to know.

I think the Reichians were megalomaniacs, true believers, and elitists. Not one of them had a bit of empathy or sympathy for children. Many of them were sadists. I really hope the truth of what happened to us becomes well known.

This is a cautionary tale about true believers and the evil that they do.

Felicia was an ex–ballet dancer and had studied under Reich. In my research for writing this book, I discovered that she also was his mistress. She had a large dark dance studio on West Seventy-Second Street. I felt scared to walk in there. Downstairs from her was a tap dance studio, where kids with no sense of rhythm made noises. I had to go up an endless flight of stairs to Felicia's studio. The tap sounds seemed to tell of the pain to come.

Her therapy was physically painful. She would stick her strong fingers into my little body until I screamed out in pain. Then she would tell me in her thick German accent that the pain was my fault because I was stiff. Reichians considered themselves to be "soft."

The third time my mother tried to send me, I grabbed the radiator and wouldn't let go. I'm proud of myself for having done that. It saved me from becoming a victim of my parents' stupidity. My sister Lucy kept going for three years.

I was also made to go to Felicia's camp for three consecutive summers from age six to eight. The name of the camp was Whispering Pines. It was a nightmare. One summer, I shared a room with two older sadistic boys, one of whom was Felicia's crazy son. They essentially beat me up every day for two months. The commotion would wake up Felicia, who would suddenly appear at the door in her see-through nightgown. It was my first view of a woman's pubic hair. As punishment, all three of us were locked in the room for most of the day. I can only remember that I saw very little of the lush countryside. My parents turned a deaf ear to my pleas of "get me out of here."

Later, my father told me that W. R. had dismissed Felicia for incompetence, so I read one of W. R.'s books entitled *The Function of the Orgasm* and enjoyed it. I wanted to understand my dad and found that we both were fascinated with the subject of sex. When I was about eighteen I had a very realistic dream where I was screwing Felicia. I woke up ejaculating. I felt that it had completely cured me of any neurosis I might have developed at her camp and studio.

For the first ten years or so of my life, I called my parents Liza and Bill. Then I started to call Bill "Daddy." I think that I wanted to remind him who I was to him. Liza remained Liza.

Two

TEEN YEARS

When I turned eleven, Liza decided I should learn another instrument. My school offered lessons in clarinet and flute. I picked the flute because it was an extension of the recorder. My teacher was Paige Brook. He had just joined the New York Philharmonic as third flute.

"It was a better gig than second flute," he said, "because I got to play first flute when the first flutist wasn't available."

Paige sent Liza and me to Albert Weatherly's at 74 West Forty-Seventh Street, where we bought a new Bundy flute for $200.

When I first heard Paige play, I realized that he was not just a teacher but a great musician. He revealed to me what he was without intimidating me. I took a lesson every week for three years. Paige was like a second father to me. Just as I learned drawing during the limited time I had with my real father, Paige brought music into my life. Sometimes I would take my flute lessons with two girls from my class, Susan Manchester and Christie MacDonald. Paige would tell us jokes, some of which were very dirty. My dad had been telling me dirty and racist jokes since he left my mother, and Paige took his place in that category too:

"What's the difference between a bull and an orchestra?"
"A bull has the horns in the front and the asshole in the rear."

Or,

"A guy is dancing with his girl and he sees that the piano player's dick is hanging out of his pants. He quickly turns his girl around so that she won't see it and dances over to the stage. 'Psst,' he says to the piano player. 'Do you know your joint's hanging out?'

"The piano player turns around and says, 'No, but if you hum the first few bars I'll try to fake it.'"

We all loved it.

Paige had met Charlie Parker. He also played great calypsos. He saw that I liked to improvise from the very beginning and encouraged it as long as I learned my classical studies first. When I had trouble sight-reading, I would try to improvise my way out of it. Paige knew every note of the music and immediately stopped me. After my first year with Paige, I had decided that I wanted to play the flute for the rest of my life.

The same year I met Paige, my father moved to Freehold, New Jersey, with his second wife, Kari. My musical father came into my life, and my art father split town. Dad let me come to see him a few times a year. I remember one visit very well. I was just going through puberty and I was jerking off every chance I got. In the afternoon while taking a bath, the hot water on my dick got me excited and I began to relieve myself. Right in the middle, I suddenly heard Kari yell to my dad, "He's masturbating!"

That night Kari decided to come in my room and tuck me in. She was wearing a flimsy nightgown and she dangled her naked breasts inches away from my face. It took all my strength not to touch the forbidden fruits.

A weaker mind could have developed a lifelong complex, but I had already decided that my stepmother was a nut. My father had told me about Kari announcing that she was going to become Reich's lover. She traveled to Maine to do just that. One fact about cults is that all the women want to fuck the leader. This case was no exception. Reich turned Kari down. My father was too valuable to give up for some pussy, so she went back to my dad. The only thing my father said when she returned was that Reich was the better man, so why wouldn't she want to be with him?

When Kari eventually left my father later, she moved down to Key West where her sister Meg lived. She ended up fucking and stealing Meg's husband. Meg committed suicide.

Seeing how serious I was about playing the flute, Liza sent me to a music camp called Indian Hill. It was there that I had my first contact with live jazz. I had been improvising, but I didn't know what to do with my new skill. The son of the camp owner was Chuck Israels, the bassist, who later played with Bill Evans. He was in a jazz quartet comprising the older kids. Perry Robinson was on clarinet, Jon Mayer was on piano, and Arnie Wise, who later also played with Bill Evans, was the drummer. The group sounded beautiful, but what impressed me the most was how the girls gravitated to them.

One day, I said to Jon Mayer, "What's a jazz tune?"

He was looking at a fake book, a book full of standards with melodies and chord symbols that jazz musicians use. He pointed to "Love Me or Leave Me" and said, "That's a jazz tune."

When I got home from camp, the same song was on the pop charts. It was sung by Lena Horne. I bought the single. Then I got all the other pop hits, which were all rock 'n' roll and I suddenly was a rock 'n' roller. I got Elvis Presley, Bill Haley, Fats Domino, and Little Richard. My question to Jon Mayer should have been "Give me the names of some good jazz musicians. I want to buy their records." Instead, I took an incredible detour, which lasted two years. My rock 'n' roll experience, however, came in handy later.

After three wonderful years with Paige, I had to go to high school. And there was only one place to go: Music and Art, which was supposed to be the best music high school in New York. My grades in middle school were terrible in everything except music, and I was sure that I would flunk out anywhere else. I practiced very hard for my entrance exam. Not knowing which part of the music I would be tested on, I learned Bach's entire B-Minor Suite. Paige told me that I had to know it 150 percent because that way I would play it 100 percent even when I became nervous. Only one out of five kids was accepted, and I made it.

In the summer of 1956, I found myself bored with rock 'n' roll—not enough chords to play over. I found a Max Roach and Clifford Brown record in a store. It sounded great, and I was determined to listen to all the other great jazz cats. I went to Camp Winooski that summer, but it wasn't as hip as Indian Hill. Everyone was into pop stuff except for one older kid named Alan. His nickname was Zorch. He brought a great collection of jazz records with him, and we listened to everybody from Miles Davis to Duke Ellington. Alan played the clarinet. He and I improvised duets together.

When I got home, I picked up the jazz magazine *DownBeat* and bought all the records that had a five-star rating with my lunch money. I rarely had lunch for the four years in high school. I read about a far-out pianist playing a steady gig at a club called the Five Spot. His name was Thelonious Monk. I asked Liza to take Zorch and me. I flipped out when I heard Monk play. John Coltrane was playing sax with him. They were incredible. That's when I knew exactly what I wanted to do with my life.

When I began my classes at Music and Art, I found that the teachers were amateurs compared to Paige. In fact, they weren't even as good as some of the students. I had a rich and intense musical experience at Indian Hill, and I thought Music and Art would be the same. I thought I might even wind up being a classical musician, but it was not meant to be. They put me in something called Intermediate Band. All we did was play marching music. I played the piccolo, and it cut through the whole band. The band had about thirty clarinet players, and the conductor worked with them most of the time—an impossible task. I was always getting in trouble for talking and making jokes.

Music and Art had four orchestras, but I was a discipline problem, so I never got to play one note of classical music. Advancement had nothing to do with how well you played, just how well you kept your mouth shut. The school had a dance band, which was full of great improvisers. An alto player named Mike Gold played very fast and smooth. Another alto, Larry Morton, also played great. Larry Willis, a fantastic piano player who is still on the scene today, was in my class. We had two terrific trumpet players: Harry Hall and Jimmy Owens. Jimmy studied with Donald Byrd. There was a guy named Joel Chenette who had his own way of playing tenor sax, but I never heard about him after school. Another tenor player, Fred Lipsius, ended up playing in Blood, Sweat & Tears. I used to try to copy his answers in geometry class.

When the New York Philharmonic went on strike, Paige told me
that his salary had gone way up after the union had won and that he
wasn't going to come to New York to teach any more. From that time,
I would take a long bus ride over the George Washington Bridge to
Dumont, New Jersey, where he lived, to continue lessons with him.
Paige built his music studio as an extension of his house. He put
in a fireplace, four chandeliers, and a grand piano. The studio had
excellent acoustics. He also built a pool in his backyard by himself. I
didn't see him every week, but I could see him when I wanted. After
a while, he stopped charging me for lessons. Meanwhile, I began
to look for friends who wanted to play jazz with me. My first jam
session was with Howie Kalish, an art student who played the guitar,
and Jonathan Schwartz, a bass player. We played over "All of Me" for
forty-five minutes. Before that, I had only played with records.

My next jazz experience was at a party in the Bronx. Abe
Mandelblatt was playing the guitar along with Larry Morton on alto.
Abe became one of my best friends at school. He also played the bass.
I would go all the way up to Mosholu Parkway in the Bronx to hang
out and play with him.

I joined the music union when I turned sixteen. I had to play a
scale to get in. The union didn't care if you could play or not; they
just took your money. I got a phone book of all the union members
and looked up jazz musicians. It was a thrill to see the names of my
heroes. Then I looked for flute players. I was still living on Charles
Street. One block uptown was Perry Street and one down was Tenth
Street. It turned out that Herbie Mann was on Perry and Bobby Jaspar
was on Tenth. Bobby was the flutist on *Kelly Blue*, a great Wynton
Kelly album. He was a terrific flute and tenor player. I had recently
heard him play with Bill Evans at Bill's first club date after he had left
Miles Davis, which was at the Show Place on West Fourth Street. I
called Bobby, and he said to come right over. He was the sweetest guy

you could ever meet. He gave me a few lessons on how to read jazz chord symbols, and we became friends.

In my junior year at Music and Art, I heard about a great thirteen-year-old bassist named Eddie Gomez who played better than Abe. We did a lot of comparing at school. There was a room full of basses at school, and that's where Eddie and I first played together. I had a copy of a tune called "Flute Bass Blues" that Bobby Jaspar had given me, which had a fast unison line played by the flute and the bass. Doug Watkins wrote it. Eddie read it perfectly, transposing by sight from G clef to bass clef. We met many times in that bass room to improvise for the five minutes between classes and often got caught playing jazz. Jazz was not respected then. I received Ns on my report card for getting caught, which stood for "not satisfactory."

As I became more occupied with school life I found it more difficult to make the long trips to Paige's. But before I completely stopped taking lessons with him, he passed on the knowledge and training exercises that he felt I needed to become a good jazz flutist. He gave me some exercise books so I would have more facility on the instrument. He told me that I should always train my ear so I could play anything I heard in my head. He also gave me vibrato exercises because he thought that a great vibrato would set me apart from the other jazz flute players.

In those days, all you had to do to play jazz was call your high school friends and invite them to your house for a jam session. On one of those occasions, I got inspired and invited Bobby Jaspar to come to my apartment to play with my high school friends. At that time, René Thomas, a great jazz guitar player from Belgium, happened to be staying with Bobby, and he brought René with him. We had just discovered a new Randy Weston tune called "Hi Fly," so we played it with them. Bobby and René showed us what real pros do with a great new tune. In the middle of the session, Jonathan Schwartz phoned me. He asked me which new record was playing in the background. I told him that it was going on live in my apartment. He couldn't believe it. Liza made us sandwiches.

One of my weekend gigs was a party at the Republican Club in New York City. Hung on the walls were two giant photos of Ike and Nixon. I asked Bobby if he could help me hire a guitar or piano player for the gig. First, he called Attila Zoller, a Hungarian guitarist, but he couldn't make it. Next, he called a pianist named Paul Bley, who took the gig. I'd never heard of him, but as soon as the gig began I knew that I was playing with a jazz giant. Listening to him play was an incredible experience. I paid him twenty bucks.

I had been trying to learn how to play alto sax so I could get more dance gigs. I played a tune on it at that gig. Paul said, "You play the flute four times better than the sax."

That night, I gave up the saxophone. Paul was a very candid person. Near the end of the gig, a dumpy obnoxious lady approached Paul and requested a tune. I clearly remember him yelling at her, "Get out of my face, bitch."

The only time the alto came in handy was when Lucy and Liza were fighting. I would go in my room, close the door, and drown out the noise by playing the sax.

Some years later, I found out that the flute fits with any kind of instrumentation. Although the flute was not a regular part of a big band, it sounded great with a big band backing it. Check out *Jazz Wave Ltd., on Tour* with the Thad Jones/Mel Lewis Orchestra.

I also worked in a marching band, which was run by a trumpet player named George Scott. The center of his lips was white from blowing so hard on his instrument. I had a pair of gray marching pants with a fat yellow stripe going down each leg. I marched down Fifth Avenue twice for two different unions on Labor Day, which paid me $15 each time, minus ten cents for the subway. As we passed

Fifty-Ninth Street, I saw a float with the Newport Youth Band playing a hot Dizzy Gillespie arrangement. They sounded great, and I wished that I were up there playing with them. I couldn't get into the band because the flute was considered a doubling instrument. All the sax players could play some flute, but I couldn't touch those guys on the sax.

George did something quite unique: he put together a jazz big band with players from the marching band, including me. The band played a concert for the prisoners at Rikers Island. We played before a packed house. You might say that we had a captive audience. For the first set, we played traditional marching band stuff, but we came back as a hip jazz band for the second. When it was my turn to take a solo, I walked across the stage to reach the microphone. The place went wild with cheers and whistling. I was a cute little kid, and they probably saw me as a piece of meat, but at the time it made me feel like a star.

I noticed that the band members knew many of the prisoners and called out to them from the stage. The prisoners were fellow musicians who had most likely been busted for drugs.

I ate the prison lunch and thought it similar to the food that was served at my school's cafeteria.

I took my flute everywhere, even to the deli. I was ready to whip it out at a moment's notice. A couple of times, I heard people playing in their apartments, and I actually knocked on the door and asked to sit in. During my high school years, dozens of coffeehouses were opening up on Bleecker, MacDougal, and Third. They all had live music. The musicians were paid by passing the hat. Living was cheap then, and you could get by on $10 a night. I sat in with everyone. I played a duo with Lou Gossett. He was a folk singer and is now known as Louis Gossett Jr., the actor. I often played with Richie Havens. I also played with Fred Neil, who later added a harmonica player to the group and paid him $1 a night. I played for free. That harmonica player was Bob Dylan. I sat in with Noel Stookey, a folk singer. He did a fantastic vocal imitation of a toilet flushing, which lasted about thirty seconds. He later became Paul of Peter, Paul and Mary. I sat in with calypso bands, beat poets, and players from the Middle East at the Café Feenjon on Seventh Avenue. The variety of music helped shape my approach to playing the flute.

In my junior year, I was offered a steady five-day-a-week job at the Commons on MacDougal Street. The spot was for a trio gig at thirty bucks a night. I wanted to use my schoolmates Leo Mitchell and Eddie Gomez. Leo was an incredible drummer. Unfortunately, Eddie's mother would not let him take the gig because of the stories she heard about Greenwich Village—my first disappointing loss of a gig. In fact, his neighborhood on 110th Street was a much more dangerous area.

Aside from the love of music, I discovered that playing on stage was indeed a good way to meet girls. Coffeehouses were nothing like today's Starbucks. The customers and waitresses knew each other. Every place had a stage. We did a lot of table-hopping. People would move from one table to another and make friends. Girls in the audience would come up to me after a good solo. Meeting girls was one of the main reasons why I wanted to be on stage.

I spent all my time after school in coffeehouses. When I wasn't playing the flute I drew pictures, played chess, and drank a lot of coffee. I was passing out at school for lack of sleep. I maintained a 67 percent average for the four years I was there. In my senior year, I completely spaced out and just did drawings in my notebooks. I went to see my grade counselor, and she told me that I couldn't get into a good college with my grades.

"That's okay. I'm going to play at the Village Vanguard," I said.

"But we don't expect you to be a musician. We just want you to be cultured," the counselor said.

"Excuse me, but isn't this a music school?"

I began to think that studying just hard enough to get by wasn't such a bad idea after all. Most of the things that were taught in school ended up as answers on television quiz shows. I missed out on being brainwashed by so-called school education because I thought I was too stupid to learn. But it turns out my insecurity about my intelligence allowed me to keep my creative brain.

I had to take four regents exams to graduate. I got a smart tutor and learned enough chemistry and English to get a 67 percent, my average. For English, I had to write about something that happened in my life. I wrote about how my mother duplicated an experiment that she read in one of Wilhelm Reich's books. It involved boiling some earth in water for six hours. After the boiling was done, Liza wrapped the earth in a cloth to make something called a bion pad, which had healing properties. Bions were supposed to contain orgone energy, which was Reich's word for qi or ether—in other words, the energy the universe swims in. She then poured the remaining water on the sweet potato plants she was growing. In a couple of days, they became a foot higher. I got an eighty-five for my English exam.

When I was down to the last exams in history and economics, my brain shut off. The Mead family was squirming over the possibility that I would fail. Uncle Richard, my mother's brother, showed up to help. He was an economics professor. I think this was the second time in my life that I saw him in person. He didn't stay long; I was burned out. It was time to say *no más*. In the morning, I left my apartment as if to go to my execution. On my way to the subway station, I bumped into a freshman girl I knew, who was on her way to school. I took her to my place and got laid. I never made it to the exams. That night I went to see the premier of the movie *Psycho*. Free at last!

Three years later, I got my first gig at the Village Vanguard.

Liza finally got a job teaching art at Lesley College in Cambridge, Massachusetts. Lucy went to live with a boyfriend. At eighteen, I had the apartment to myself. I met a beautiful thirty-six-year-old waitress at Figaro's on Bleecker Street. We lived together for three months. She told me that she once had an affair with my Uncle Arthur. I liked knowing that he was not as pure as he made himself out to be.

I landed a job as a microfilm trainee in the Wall Street area. My first assignment was to microfilm the *National Enquirer*. I was paid $1 an hour. My wages were supposed to increase to $1.50 after a month of training. When the month was up, they told me that I wasn't ready for the raise, so I quit. Then I went to work for a savings and loan association as an office boy. In the evening, I went to nightclubs to listen to jazz. The Village Gate was my favorite jazz joint. The Horace Silver Quintet played every Monday. The energy of the group was unbelievable. John Coltrane would often play there too. I could see his notes cascading from the bell of his horn.

Herbie Mann performed with his Afro-Cuban group. He had three great percussionists: Ray Mantilla and Ray Barretto on the congas and Babatunde Olatunji on the drums. Dave Pike, Herbie's vibes player whom I had met at the Cafe Wha?, said he would ask Herbie if I could sit in. The next time I showed up at the Gate, Dave asked, but Herbie said the band needed to work on some new material and wouldn't let me play. On my next visit, he said the place was too full. Herbie finally agreed to let me play when the audience had about five people. As we headed for the bandstand, he asked me if I had my union card. I showed it to him. As we got closer to the stage, he asked me if I had my cabaret card. In those days, musicians couldn't work unless they were fingerprinted and given an ID. I showed him my cabaret card. I think he really didn't want me on the stage.

We played "St. Thomas" by Sonny Rollins. I waited for everyone to play before I took a solo. Herbie took a second solo with the congas. That was it. I wished I could have soloed with the congas—I loved the two Rays. I recorded with both of them many years later.

The next day I called Bobby Jaspar and told him what had happened. Bobby said, "I'm playing at the Village Vanguard with my quartet. Come down and you can play the whole set with me."

He had a group called the International Quartet with Eddie de Haas, the bass player from Holland; Attila Zoller, the Hungarian guitarist; and Edgar Bateman, the American drummer. I enjoyed myself much more because Bobby was happy to have me there. I must add that with age, Herbie became mellow and less competitive. About twenty-five years later, I sat in with him again at Fat Tuesday's. He turned me on to a dynamite joint.

I met my first wife at Herbie's gig. I was into *Playboy* magazine, and she had a Playboy figure except that she was bowlegged, which

I thought was pretty cute. I took her home, and she never left until our divorce. Of course, we had to get married first. I was nineteen and she was seventeen.

Christmas came, and she said to me, "I put something in your coffee. It's something like pot."

We drank the coffee, and thirty minutes later, we broke out into hysterical laughter. We ran through the streets to get to an apartment where we had been house-sitting for the holidays. On the way there, the buildings looked like undulating sponges. Once we reached the apartment, I found myself in a different world. She had given me psilocybin, the active ingredient in magic mushrooms—a very powerful psychedelic drug. Streaks of blue and pink energy filled the room. I fell down on my back while laughing. Some of my visions were frightening, but the laughter made it easier to accept what I was seeing. For example, I looked up at the cracks in the ceiling, which appeared as worms crawling over each other. I felt as though

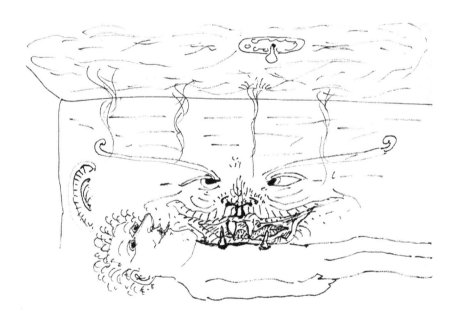

I had microscopic vision. Everything was super clear and realer than real. Cracks in the wall looked like the marching trees in the movie *Fantasia*. I could see everything in my hands, including the blood flowing through my veins. I asked her if I would ever come down and be normal again. She assured me that I would. The trip and laughter lasted about eight hours until I began to come down. I sat by the fireplace feeling completely emptied out. After that experience, I told her that I didn't need any dope in my life. I had tried pot only once, and I was very much against drugs at that time.

She and I didn't really know each other. We had sex and read books together. I worked as an office boy for the rest of our time together. After we broke up, I found out that she had been cheating on me for the six months we were together. Her last words to me were "You can shove Wilhelm Reich up your ass."

I wasn't ready for marriage until my fifth one at the age of sixty.

Three

FLUTE FEVER

Trude Heller's was a nightclub on Ninth Street and Sixth Avenue. I would sit in with Morgana King, who later played the role of the wife of Vito Corleone in the movie *The Godfather*. She was singing with the guitarist Jim Hall. Knobby Totah was the bass player. Billy Bean used to work around the corner from the club and often came over and played guitar duos with Jim.

Trude, the owner of the club, was a tough dyke. She gave me my first nightclub date. I was to play with Jim and Knobby. Jim was already a jazz legend back then. On the week of the gig, I didn't think I was playing that well. The week after the gig, however, I found my playing had greatly improved. The process of learning through playing with seasoned musicians takes a while to set in.

After seeing me draw on paper napkins at the club, Trude gave me my first art show on her walls. While my pictures were still up, I read in the papers that Katharine Hepburn had bought one of them. I ran over to Trude's to find out which one she had bought. Trude explained to me that the papers had lied and that it was only publicity.

Trude gave me some good advice, which I wish I had listened to. She told me to always look slick no matter how down and out I might really be. Instead, I ended up becoming a long-haired hippie.

One night, I met Tadd Dameron at Trude's. He was a very friendly guy. I told him that my goal was to be one of the real jazz guys whose photos I had pasted on my wall. He told me that I already was. Trude Heller's closed years ago and was replaced by a pizza joint.

On Mondays, I would go over to Page Three, a lesbian hangout, down the street from my apartment. I would sit in with the band and listen to Sheila Jordan sing in a duo with Steve Swallow on upright bass. I hired Steve and Paul Bley to play a steady Sunday afternoon gig at a club called Phase Two. Gary Peacock would substitute for Steve when he couldn't make it. When Paul couldn't make it, his wife, Carla, would play. I think I learned the most by playing with Carla because she was an excellent composer. Her tunes were modern and sounded great on the flute. One time, Paul and Steve played "Oleo" so fast that they left me in the dust. It didn't bother me too much; I was still a kid and had a lot to learn. I liked the tune and recorded it on my first album.

Another memorable gig was with Teddy Kotick. I met him when he was playing with Joe Roland, the vibes player, at a club called Top of the Mountain on Eighth Street. Teddy had played with Charlie Parker and Billie Holiday. I felt amazed that I was able to meet and play with all these musicians who had incredible connections to jazz history just by walking into joints and asking if I could play with them. Teddy invited me to play at a club in Staten Island with Vinnie

Ruggieri, Hod O'Brien, Jim Hall, and Tal Farlow. To listen to Jim play with Tal while I was playing with them was very special. All these musicians I was playing with at the nightclubs almost on a daily basis were mature and much more advanced than I, but they accepted me. I don't see this kind of openness anymore.

The musicians were also open about themselves. For example, I learned that Vinnie liked to get high on a cough syrup called Cosanyl. It was no secret. Cosanyl was loaded with codeine, and you had to sign for it at the counter. If you tried to buy too much, you would get in trouble. On the night of the Staten Island gig, Vinnie told me a funny story. His father was a barber at the Waldorf Astoria. One day Vinnie walked in, and his dad was cutting the Duke of Windsor's hair. The duke said to Vinnie, "If there is anything I can do for you, just ask."

Vinnie had him sign for a bottle of Cosanyl.

I had a chance to do a demonstration recording, and Teddy offered to help me put it together. He brought Vinnie, Hod, and himself as my rhythm section. The recording came out very well. My uncle Henry made a phone call to John Hammond, a producer at Columbia Records. He had read Henry's jazz novel, and that was how he knew my uncle. I went to meet with him and play the demo tape for him. John Hammond was the father of my school chum John Hammond Jr., whose nickname from school was Jeep, short for John Paul. We went to Little Red School House in the Village together in first grade. However, I wasn't aware of that coincidence because Jeep lived with his mother when we were kids.

Hammond Sr. seemed to like my demo tape and said that they might do something with me. I was still working as an office boy, and I took the acetate to the Christmas party at the office so my fellow workers could hear it. The next day, my boss fired me. She said that I was clearly going to be doing something else for a living and that my heart wasn't in office work. So, I was a failure as an office boy, but she must have liked the music. I was almost twenty, and it was time that I tried to become a paid musician.

In the spring of 1962, I went to Bermuda with a band made up of college kids. The group was strictly an amateur band, but that trip changed my life forever. We were there over Easter vacation, and the island was alive with college kids having a good time getting drunk. I made two discoveries on that trip. One was that the best way to pick up a girl was to smile at her. The other was how good my hearing was. I could hear everyone in the band and all the conversations at the dinner tables. Little did I know that I was about to lose both my smile and great hearing.

The only way to get around the island was by motorbike, and you didn't need a license to rent one. I loved my motorbike. I rode it all over the island. Since everyone was drinking, I began drinking myself. I was talking very loudly, and our table in the hotel dining room kept getting moved until we were the last table in the back.

Bermuda was a paradise. The beaches were filled with beautiful young women. In the day, the water was rich blue, and at night, the sky showed a million huge stars. I sat in with all the bands on the island and felt that my life was going through a big change. It seemed that everything I played was brand new. My playing was getting much stronger.

Two weeks later, it was time to go home. I decided to take one more ride on my beloved motorbike. Unfortunately, they had never given me a helmet to go with the bike.

I was riding, and suddenly I was in dreamland—one dream after another. I was going to big jam sessions on the island and playing my best solos ever. I was getting laid, and the party never seemed to end.

The strange thing was that I wouldn't wake up at the end of each dream. I'd black out instead. Then I'd wake up into another dream. This seemed to go on forever, and I finally realized that I would die if I didn't wake up. I summoned all my strength and woke up in the hospital.

My wrists were strapped down with leather belts, but I somehow fell out of bed and began to crawl toward the door. The doctors found me and put me back in bed. I had been in a coma for ten days. The next thing I remember was seeing my father, Lucy, her soon-to-be husband, Edi, and my little half-sister, Maggie (four years old), standing around my bed. I needed physical contact and asked them to hold my feet, which helped a lot. (I recommend that technique to head injury victims; it is a good way to reconnect with the outside world.) I had been kicked out of intensive care for trying to grab the nurses, which I didn't remember at all. To me, my entire stay was all a dream.

My mother was on vacation in Florence, Italy, for the summer. I didn't ask to let her know because I didn't want to ruin her trip. My father wasn't going to tell her anyway. That nobody told her until she returned from Italy made her really angry. I guess I didn't see it from her point of view.

I fell into a deep sleep again, which continued for another week, and woke up in the middle of the night. I had bars around my bed, and it looked as if I were in a diner. A very pretty nurse from Arizona looked to me like a waitress in her white uniform. She said, "Is there anything I can do for you?"

"Yes, give me a hotdog with sauerkraut," I said.

She reminded me that I was in the hospital. After that I rejoined reality. Every time I laughed at something funny, I felt a painful jolt in my head. The extent of the damage from the motorbike accident sank in slowly. At first I noticed that I had double vision. My eyes wouldn't work together. I saw two of everything. The two images overlapped, and reality was somewhere in between. I had to cover one eye to eat my food. My left eye wouldn't close, and it would roll up when I went to sleep. The eyeball didn't get enough lubrication, causing an ulcerated cornea. They put medicine on it and gave me an eye patch, which also helped me see where things were. I had a big bandage around my head and caked blood in both ears. The doctor told me I had fractured my skull.

To this day, I don't know how the accident happened. I have no memory of the event. I know that I was drinking, and I think that it was probably my fault. My father was very sweet to me while I was in the hospital. I couldn't see well enough to read, so he read me a book by Ludwig Bemelmans, a writer for the *New Yorker*. The novel was about working as a waiter in hotel restaurants. I learned that the fancier the place, the more likely the food had been dropped on the floor and dusted off. Bemelmans said that he would only eat where he could see the food being prepared.

Three weeks into my consciousness, two attendants carried me to the restroom in the hall. I happened to look at a mirror on the way and learned something new. The left half of my face was totally paralyzed. A few days later, I got another shock. I was told that I would never hear in my left ear again. I cried, but the tears would come out of only my right eye.

I had two main worries: If I couldn't play the flute anymore, how was I going to have a creative life? And how was I going to ever get laid again with my distorted face? I wanted to draw, but my hands were numb and I couldn't hold a pen. I used to hold it with my forefinger wrapped around my thumb, which was something I've never seen anyone else do. This method gave me a great deal of control. Now I would have to relearn everything, including walking, which my body had forgotten how to do.

My father bought me painting crayons called Payons. When dipped in water, they would spread color easily. I started to draw holding the Payons at the ends with my fingertips, and to this day, that's the way I hold a pen. This technique makes it a little harder to control the lines, but they come out much looser, and I could have a better view of the paper while drawing.

I stayed at the hospital for about six weeks, and then they wheeled me in a wheelchair to my first jet plane. The next step in my recovery was spending three weeks in a hospital in Waterbury, Connecticut. American doctors love to test for abnormalities. They gave me my second spinal tap. The first was in Bermuda. I was told that it would make me feel better but in fact caused the worst pain I've ever experienced. The procedure was done in three stages. First, I was given a painful pain-killing shot in the ass cheek. That set me up for an even more painful Novocain shot in the spine. And finally they stuck a needle in my spine and drew out fluid. Knowing the pain I was going to experience, a skinny, homely nurse with a pronounced limp held my hands for the ordeal, which got me through it and for that moment I was in love.

I went through many painful tests. An electroencephalograph measured my brain waves, which involved wires attached to my head with little pins. I also had an isotope brain scan, which required me to lie on my back, both sides, and finally my face for two hours each without moving. Boy, did my nose hurt for those last two hours.

I had another test where I was put to sleep, and a tube was inserted down my throat. When I came to, a heavy-set, pimply nurse brought me my dinner. I told her that I didn't feel like eating in my condition at the time, but she went ahead and lifted the cover off the food to reveal chicken and asparagus. I rolled over and puked my guts out. Years later, I did finally acquire a taste for asparagus.

The tests revealed nothing, and I refused to take any more. I never knew what they were looking for in the first place. I was only concerned with my face. The ear was finished. The nerve had been severed. The head neurosurgeon came to me with a suggestion: they could fix my face with a little plastic surgery. They wanted to lift the paralyzed side of my face into a permanent smile. I said to my dad, "Get me out of here."

We heard about a doctor in Montreal who was doing one of the earlier operations with microscopes. I took my second jet to Canada and booked into the Royal Victoria Hospital. The whole place was beautiful. My room was like a nice hotel room, and it had a television. I had had countless X-rays in Connecticut, but this new doctor, Holly McCue, knew his stuff and only needed two X-rays to see exactly what had happened to my face. I had bone chips stuck in my facial nerve. He ordered an operation immediately. The night before the operation, I watched *Perry Mason* and *Ben Casey* (a hospital favorite) on television. After the operation, I was unconscious forever. I woke up for a minute, peed a full quart and passed out again. When I woke up again, I filled another quart bottle. It must have been the intravenous.

My dad had a friend in Montreal whose name was Grad. He was supposedly a scientist, doing very interesting experiments with a Hungarian healer named Estebani. In Hungary, healing was a respected practice until the Russians invaded and messed the country up. Grad had done experiments with Reich's orgone box, which was made of organic and metallic layers and was supposed to trap life energy inside, and he tried to re-create them using Estebani's own innate energy.

I saw photographs of some of his experiments. In one, Grad would present Estebani with two sets of plants. Estebani would pass his hands over one set and leave the other alone. The treated plants all grew a few inches higher than the untreated ones. In another experiment, Estebani put his hands around a bottle of water. Again, he tested two sets of plants: one was watered with ordinary water and the other with treated water. The latter grew higher. Grad and Dad snuck Estebani into my hospital room after my facial nerve surgery. He put his hands on my head. I don't know if it helped, but his hands were very warm.

When I left the hospital, I went to live with my dad for two months. This was the first time I lived with him after he left me when I was three. My father was in the process of breaking up with Kari. The atmosphere was pretty tense, and I sometimes wished I was back in the hospital. Kari could hold her liquor, but she was drinking as much as a pint of whiskey a day and was pretty mean to my dad. She tried to emasculate him by calling him an old man. He fought back with dry humor. They weren't easy to be around.

Being in the middle of my father's divorce wasn't helping me recover, so I went back to the apartment on Charles Street. Not knowing if I would ever play the flute again, I tried to set up alternatives. I tacked large canvases to the wall and began to paint. I went up to Forty-Eighth Street and rented a studio with some vibes in it. I was a natural flute player but sucked on vibes, so I scratched the idea of becoming a vibes player.

To keep my facial muscles from atrophying, I had to go to Saint Vincent's Hospital for treatments. They would send small electric shocks through my face to keep the muscles alive. One day as I was getting ready for a treatment, my friend Zorch from camp showed up with Hassan Ibn Ali, a pianist, whom he wanted me to meet. Hassan had just finished recording with Max Roach. Zorch was excited to hook up with a real jazz musician, but for some reason he immediately split, leaving me with one of the craziest people I've ever met.

Hassan stayed in my pad for almost twenty-four hours, during which time he shot up smack every thirty minutes. Doing junk is a very messy process. Hassan bled all over my apartment. Every time I tried to get him out of my place, he would shoot up again or clean his false teeth. He finally left the next day. I have never met anyone who had anything good to say about him.

Looking back, I'm certain that my friend Zorch simply needed a place to dump him. Elmo Hope, the great bebop pianist, told me a Hassan story. The police banged on Hassan's door. Instead of throwing his drugs out the window, he hid them on the window ledge of the bathroom and closed the window. Of course, he got busted. One of Hassan's tunes was called "Hope So, Elmo."

It took six months to feel any movement on the left side of my face, and I didn't get back what I'd hoped for. My facial muscles were pretty weak, and I couldn't uncover my upper or lower teeth on the left side. I couldn't blow through the middle of my mouth because the left side was too weak to hold together. I thought my flute-playing days were over.

One day, I went to see my dad at the Marlton Hotel on West Eighth Street. Kari had just thrown him out of the house. In their last attempt at reconciliation, Dad and Kari went on a skiing trip. For some reason I'll never understand, they took Elmer, a friend of my father's, along. Elmer boasted of having slept with three hundred women, which impressed my father a great deal. According to my father, Elmer screwed Kari during the trip, and that spelled the end of their marriage. Dad went into a deep depression. To try to snap him out of it, I said to him, "How would you like to see your daddy shackled in the public square getting his naked ass whipped?"

That worked well, and he began to look for another woman. He thanked me for saying that many times that year.

That same day, my father reached in the drawer and took out my flute. He had brought it with him from the country. I hadn't taken it back with me to New York because I didn't expect to play again.

"Try and play it," he said.

"I can't, Dad. Not enough muscles."

He insisted that I show him what I could do with it. I held one hand over the left side of my mouth and played a few notes with the other. Then it came to me—I grabbed a matchbook, tore it in half, and placed it under my lips in front of my teeth on the left side of my mouth. I could still make the flute embouchure, and the cardboard prevented the air from pushing the weak side of my mouth open. Suddenly, as if by magic, I could play. It lasted twenty seconds. Then the cardboard became soggy and blew out of my mouth across the room. But I had played for twenty seconds. The Wright brothers' first flight lasted only twelve seconds. I knew I could find a way to perfect it.

I took a shirt cardboard and cut out about fifty mouthpieces and went to a piano bar uptown with them. I took out my flute and laid all the mouthpieces in front of me on a piece of paper and asked the pianist if I could sit in. By the time I used the last cardboard, the first one was dry. I had a new lease on life. Soon I improved the mouthpiece by wrapping plastic tape around it and shaping it to the inside of my mouth.

I called Bobby Jaspar. I had a vision that we should have a two-flute band. When I got him on the phone, he was very sick and was about to go into the hospital for heart surgery. His girlfriend told me that he had had a terrible experience there. Another patient in his room was screaming and crying with pain all night. In a moment of frustration, Bobby said, "Why don't you die already?" The next day, the guy was dead, and Bobby felt awful.

I decided to see Bobby after his operation when he would be feeling better. I'll always regret that decision. Bobby didn't survive the operation. My first idea of getting back in the scene ended tragically.

In the summer of 1963, I heard from Al Oehrle, one of the guys I had played with during the Bermuda gig. He was going to Europe on a Holland America Line ship with another college band and asked me to join them. The gig was my first after breaking my head. The ship was filled with seven hundred kids of my age, and I spent my time playing the flute and running after girls. After the ship hit the high seas, there was no liquor tax, and a bottle of Heineken was eleven cents. I learned to chug-a-lug, which was to drink a full bottle of beer without stopping. I chug-a-lugged seven bottles in a row and got quite drunk. I ended up holding on to the railing at the end of the ship. I was very lucky not to have fallen into the ocean.

Jazz was big in Europe, and I thought we could get gigs there, but the guys in the band weren't really musicians. They all had other aspirations and only played on the boat to get to Europe for free. When we arrived in Amsterdam, they split and became tourists. Al rented a car, and I went with him. When we stopped in Nice on the French Riviera, I met an Israeli girl and made out with her behind a beached fishing boat on a bed of small pebbles. I was too excited to notice that my arm was getting numb. When I got up, I couldn't move my wrist. The next day, my arm didn't feel any better and I went to the hospital there to get it checked out. The doctors thought something was wrong with my heart. When a person is experiencing heart trouble they sometimes feel a numbness in the hands. I couldn't deal with that. They didn't speak English, and I knew that it really had to do with the pebbles on the beach. Fortunately, Liza was on her summer vacation in Florence, and I had just enough money to get there. I went on a beautiful twenty-hour train trip passing Monaco and lots of coastal cities like Pisa.

Liza was staying in a *pensione* across from the Boboli Gardens, a magnificent place. We went to outdoor cafés every day and drank cognac and beer, my mom's favorite turn-on. She had a great memory for what she saw. She would go back to the *pensione* and re-create on canvas the places where we had been. We visited many museums. We saw the *Birth of Venus* in the shell at the Uffizi Gallery and works by Luca Della Robbia at another. We went way up in the hills to see the Fra Angelico Museum. Fra Angelico painted with egg tempera, which lasts much longer than oil. The paintings looked almost new. Liza and I drank in Michelangelo Square. Liza was an alcoholic and often was confused, but when it came to art, she was very knowledgeable. I learned a lot about my mom in the month we spent together in Florence and gained new respect for her.

My wrist was still numb, but as luck would have it, a Hungarian lady came to my rescue. Her name was Dr. Yaila Brichter. She was about seventy-five and staying down the hall from us. She gave me a wonderful what I'd call "cosmic massage." She also showed me relaxing exercises while I was there. She would have me sit in a chair with my eyes closed and tell me to relax in a very soothing Hungarian accent. She had me concentrate on relaxing various parts of my body, starting from the top of my head. She would say, "Think of the space between your eyes and relax it," and so forth. By the time I focused on my shoulders, I was already breathing much more comfortably.

I caught the train from Florence to Paris. I had taken two terms of French in high school, but I didn't remember anything. I didn't take the classes seriously because I never thought that I would get out of the United States. In other words, I was a typical American. On the subway, I looked at the map for a recognizable stop. I found two: the Bastille and the Louvre. I chose the Louvre. I found a room for $1 a night about a block from the museum and went to sleep. I woke up to all kinds of noises from outside. I looked out the window and realized that I was in the middle of the main food marketplace.

I spent three days in Paris letting myself get lost. The city had so many landmarks and famous buildings, and, of course, the Eiffel

Tower could be seen from anywhere. Being alone with no one to talk to, I was in a meditative state. I walked to the Louvre. The museum was enormous, and I never made it out of the Egyptian section to see the impressionists. Paris was beautiful.

I found a club where Chet Baker was playing and sat in with him. He let me play in the ensemble parts. I hadn't met him before that night, but he let me join anyway. I also saw Bud Powell play just before his death. He could barely play, but I enjoyed seeing him in person. He was an important part of jazz history.

I took the boat back to the United States from Amsterdam. The most amazing sight that happens on the ocean is the sunrise and the sunset. You just have to see them for yourself. I will never forget that summer.

Back in New York, I was summoned for my army physical. The Vietnam War was heating up. Standing in line with fifty other naked men didn't make me want to pass the exam. I had my first blood test—the first one I was aware of. I watched as the blood filled the syringe and suddenly became pale. When I came out of the room, a bunch of new recruits laughed at me and said, "What's the matter? Didn't eat your breakfast?"

If they had known where they were headed, they would have skipped breakfast and more. I didn't pass because of my deaf ear. The great pianist Wynton Kelly also had a deaf ear, but the army took him anyway. I heard from Jimmy Cobb that they didn't believe he was deaf because he played so well.

I saw Jeep singing at the Fat Black Pussycat Café on MacDougal Street. He had become a blues singer. (Later, Hammond Sr. told me that his son had no right to sing the blues because he was white.) We hadn't seen each other since we were little kids, and the reunion was nice. He reintroduced me to pot, which helped alleviate the headaches I had been experiencing since the accident. I also found that pot made it easier to hear through my one functioning ear. We would smoke pot in the red-painted bathroom in the basement of his apartment and play the blues upstairs afterward. He had all the great classic records and introduced me to just about everyone from Bo Diddley to Howlin' Wolf.

I remember the first time I tried to buy pot. I paid $20 for it and took it over to Jeep's. He told me that I had been swindled—it was

catnip. We went into his backyard, and he sprinkled it on the ground. In two minutes, about thirty cats were rolling all over the grass in complete happiness.

Having learned how to play the flute with a mouthpiece, I had many new ideas. I called John Hammond Sr. to tell him that I had had an accident but was back in shape again. He gave me a record deal. I tried to get Sam Brown to play the guitar and Hod O'Brien the piano, but Hammond wanted to choose the band himself. He hired Denny Zeitlin, who turned out to be a very hot piano player, with Ben Tucker on bass and Ben Riley on drums. I practiced for the recording by playing with records such as *Everybody Digs Bill Evans* and Miles Davis's *In Person Friday Night at the Blackhawk*.

The night before the recording, I was so excited with anticipation that I couldn't sleep. The next morning I dragged my tired ass up to Columbia's Thirtieth Street studio to make my first album. We used the very first take of the first tune that we recorded, which was "Blue Seven" by Sonny Rollins. The session lasted only three hours. I played well, but Hammond ignored me for the entire time I was there.

By this time, I had found out what a mean, insensitive person my producer was. He refused to talk to me and treated Denny as if it were his record. He'd say things like "Denny, what's the next tune?" without ever acknowledging my presence. At the end of the recording date, he asked me to be coleaders with Denny.

"I-I-th-th-think y-y-you should share the record with Denny and split the royalties."

He had an annoying stutter, but the last part came out really fast with no stutter. In essence, he was trying to take the record, *Flute Fever*, away from me.

"No," I said—the best one-word sentence I ever spoke in my life.

I haven't received a dime since I was paid $328 for recording the album and drawing the cover. That Hammond Jr. and I went to school together probably affected the way he treated me. He even put my real first name on the record, even though I was known as Jemmy. He said that Jemmy was a girl's name because his ex-wife was called Jemmy for Jemison.

I was straight for the recording of my first album. Playing was fun up until then, but in the music business, you have to deal with many unmusical nonmusicians. Hammond Sr. was one of them. I wasn't ready for the psychological games he played with me. I thought that I needed to smoke at my future recordings so I could concentrate on the music.

Dave Lambert, of the singing group Lambert, Hendricks & Ross, gave me some good tips on how to conduct myself as a pothead. You have to come to the gig straight and not get high until just before the second set. He had a little wooden pipe and showed me how to cap it with a pack of matches. This was his technique: he would go into a booth in the bathroom, light up, take one draw off the pipe, and cap it with the matchbook. Then he would keep sucking in air and hold his breath until all the smoke was absorbed in his lungs. This way, smells never lingered. He'd finish off by popping a mint into his mouth, and it was show time. I used this technique from time to time, but after a while, I smoked openly in the dressing rooms and recording studios. People were much looser about pot before the United States launched a war on drugs. Now if people smoke, they do so privately and in secret.

Some good things happened during my affiliation with old man Hammond. He took me up to Harlem to sit in with George Benson. I also played a party at Hammond's house with an all-star band, which included Dizzy Gillespie, Stan Getz, Sam Brown, and Ray Bryant. Stan had just gotten married to a Scandinavian beauty queen. She was at the party and heard me play. She said to Stan, "Why don't you let him sit in with you at the Vanguard?"

I played with Stan that week. I remember playing "Airegin," a tune by Sonny Rollins. Stan got up to the microphone and said, "How do you like that? He's only sixteen years old."

Flute Fever was a tremendous leap from sitting in with musicians at coffeehouses and clubs and playing over my record collection. Today, fifty years after it came out, I can't bear to listen to it. I hear the mistakes and a few out-of-tune notes. However, I get inquiries from people who want to get a digital copy of the album all the time. They seem to love the album while showing no interest in what I did after I had learned my craft. A digital copy is not available.* Sony bought Columbia and pressed five thousand CD copies of the album. Then they realized they needed my permission to release it. Being older and wiser, I asked Sony how much they were going to pay me. They said, "Nothing."

"How about $50?" I asked jokingly.

The answer was no. Sony even advertised the album's release before contacting me. Now they have five thousand CDs in their warehouse somewhere, and people who have seen the advertisement keep writing to me. My first big career move never earned me anything.

I kept asking Hammond Sr. how I could get some paying gigs. I would sit with him in his office and wait for hours until he talked to me. Every time I started to open my mouth, he'd make a phone call or make me listen to one of his records and grin at me. Finally, he hooked me up with Paul Winter. Paul met with me for lunch and played one of his records for me called *Jazz Meets the Bossa Nova*. His pianist Warren

---

* In 2013, *Flute Fever* came out on CD, digitally remastered.

Bernhardt had arranged a bunch of beautiful Brazilian songs. The record sounded pretty good, so I decided to join the band.

I don't remember ever having a good time with the band. Warren was the only guy whom I enjoyed playing with. He was an excellent pianist. Unfortunately, 90 percent of the gig was reading music, and I was frustrated not being able to play jazz. I was given one feature tune with a single chord to play over. What's more, Paul made us wear ugly gray suits. Mine was passed down from the guy who had been in the band before me.

The concerts were held in large halls filled with people who were eager to listen to jazz. Every time I stepped onto the stage, I thought that we were going to do something musical, but reality always set in. Paul always played the same solo. We weren't a jazz band—we were a show masquerading as one.

The road trips were the hardest I've ever been on. We'd drive to Florida nonstop for twenty hours, do the gig, and drive back the next morning. We did a tour of the South for three weeks and played every night. Warren advised me on how to stretch my money by existing on hamburgers and malteds. I made about $600 in total and had to pay my expenses out of that. At that time, the hotels were only $5 to $10 a night, and I came home with $90. That was my rent. We drove over four thousand miles, but the trip wasn't too bad because I stayed high smoking pot in Warren's car the whole time.

On another trip, we played opposite Peter, Paul and Mary in a huge benefit for Lyndon Johnson to save us from Barry Goldwater. Mary gave me a back rub after the concert, which is one source of relief as I look back. All the liberal musicians were playing in support of Johnson because they thought that he would get us out of Vietnam, but he paid everyone back by escalating the war. I never trust politicians. I made up for the mistake of playing that gig by joining a number of anti-Vietnam War benefits on my own.

When we played a festival in Daytona Beach, Bill Evans dropped by at the hotel. Warren was a good friend of his. Bill and his wife, Elaine, were in Florida, kicking drugs together. Bill was very candid about his habit. He told me that he was eating breakfast one day, and two teeth fell out in the scrambled eggs. That's when he decided to clean up.

I had my girlfriend with me. The five of us hung out every day. We went to Marineland and saw a seal play "Pop Goes the Weasel" on squeeze trumpets with its mouth.

Bill wasn't just a musical genius; he was good at everything. We went bowling together, and Bill won all the games. He took my girl-friend to the driving range. She said that he was consistently hitting over two hundred yards. We shot pool, and Bill ran the table three times right away. He knew how to put English on the ball, and the cue ball would always stop in front of the ball he wanted to hit next. He said that he had learned pool in the Boy Scouts.

At the end of the trip, my girlfriend said that she wanted to get married. I didn't know why, but I was crazy about her, so I said, "Yes."

She was a Playboy Bunny, and I was an idiot.

Shortly after the trip, I married my bunny at a chapel in New York. She had a mini wedding dress on and a dozen white roses in her hands. My father bought me one of Wilhelm Reich's orgone boxes for a wedding present. We didn't have a honeymoon because I left for Oklahoma with the Paul Winter band for a week in a nightclub. The next day, my new bride called me with the news that I had crabs.

"What's that?" I asked.

"Look at your balls," she screamed.

I did and saw a small dot on my testicles. I scratched at it, and it sprung legs and began running away. Not having any experience with those things, I didn't realize for a while that the bunny had given me the crabs. I went to the drug store. I was embarrassed, to say the least, and in a very low timid voice asked the lady behind the counter if she had something for crabs. She left for a minute and then shoved a box of Midol in my face.

"Not cramps, crabs," I said in a much louder voice that surprised me.

She then took out something for crabs. Freddie Waits, the drummer in Paul's band, later told me A200 was the best stuff to use to get rid of crabs.

One good thing happened that week: I finally played jazz with Warren. The owner of the club kept the place open after the gig, and Warren and I jammed with the house band. They were smokers and grew their own marijuana. They drove us out into the country and after a short walk showed us two giant plants, which were about seven feet tall.

After Oklahoma, the band went to Miami. I called my wife, but she was not home, so I called my dad, who had moved into an apartment on Washington Place in the Village. My wife answered the phone.

"Hi, Jem, I just turned your father on."

Then my dad got on the phone, and he sounded quite different.

"Hi, Jemmy, this stuff is wonderful. We've been hugging."

"That's nice," I said.

I could never get my father to tell me what had really happened that night. I tried to catch him every twenty years or so, but he wouldn't talk about it. The bunny and I lasted another six months until she ran off with Tim Hardin.

A big historical event happened while we were married. John F. Kennedy was gunned down. The news of the assassination took over the television for three or four days, but most of the coverage was of the funeral. When Jack Ruby shot Lee Harvey Oswald in front of the whole country on television, I was sure that the assassination had to be a conspiracy, as did any other intelligent person. I read the papers from top to bottom for months expecting to read investigative reports, but I found none. Oswald was declared the lone assassin, and all news about Kennedy disappeared. Had my country been taken over with no one noticing? I started then to get suspicious, but it would be decades before I looked back and wondered if it had anything to do with my world of jazz.

One day, Jeep took me to the Bitter End Coffeehouse to see a jug band. A member of the band had some pure mescaline, and Jeep and I took a dose in my apartment. It was very powerful. I remember putting *Flute Fever* on. My reaction was "That's how I'm going to sound when I grow up." I had regressed to about six years old. Jeep went outside to see the world, but I was paranoid and afraid to leave my apartment. I thought that the police would arrest me if they saw my dilated pupils. All the bad memories from my childhood came back. I finally went to sleep worrying that I would swallow my tongue.

This bad mescaline trip and a year with Paul Winter had cut me off from my musical brain. I was more aware than ever of the handicap of my deafness. For the first two years after breaking my head, I retained the memory of hearing in my left ear. It reminded me of going to bed on my side yet knowing that the ear pushed against the pillow still functions. After the mescaline trip, I lost that memory, and I dare say a few brain cells went with it. I lost my edge on music for two or three years. I had no problem playing with Paul Winter, as very little improvising was required.

Paul's next gig was in Brazil. I was fed up with the music, but I wanted to see Brazil, so I went. Rio de Janeiro is a very beautiful place, with pristine beaches surrounded by big mountains, incredible sunrises and sunsets, and a lot of sweet but totally unreliable people. Everyone smoked reefer, and the weed was powerful. I hung out with a bunch of Brazilian musicians. On my first night in Rio, three local musicians and I toured around Rio in an old car. We stopped by a giant waterfall at about two in the morning. We parked by a bridge, which was about fifty feet high over a stream. One of the musicians stood on the ledge and began to pee. The other two followed suit. Then, they turned to me and said, "Brazilian pee, you must pee."

I was stoned out of my gourd and could hardly walk. I also have a fear of heights but still considered the challenge. Just then, the police showed up. They knew where people went to smoke. I found four or five policemen standing in front of my face. I had a very fair complexion, and my face was still paralyzed on the left side.

"His face is crazy. His face is crazy," one of the cops kept saying, while my fellow musicians tried their best to explain my paralysis in Portuguese. The cops didn't find the pot and disappeared as fast as they had appeared. The weed was hidden under our car seat—we lucked out big time.

Paul was pretty good at booking his own gigs, but the band's concerts for the first three weeks didn't happen. We had to fend for ourselves. I had a hotel room in Ipanema, but I had only $10, though it wasn't as bad as it sounds. At that time, you could get yourself a tuxedo for $25 in Brazil. I survived on ham and cheese sandwiches and fruit juices, which I loved, especially the avocado milk shake. Fruit drink stands were on every block. I was becoming weaker every day from excessive smoking and poor diet.

Halfway through the trip with Paul, I was sitting on a park bench drawing pictures when a pack of small kids surrounded me. *What nice looking kids!* I thought. Then one of them grabbed my alto flute. I grabbed it back. Another reached in my pocket and took my drawing pen, so I got up to chase him. He then waved a knife at me, so I went back to the hotel. Recently I saw a story on television about bands of children in Brazil who were using the same kind of tactics on tourists. The difference is that now they actually slice the victim's clothes off, and people are helpless to stop it.

During the last week of our stay, we played opposite Connie Francis. I also did a record for Gilberto Gil and made $10. I wanted to get my own stash of weed. Tonario, a terrific local pianist, took me to the mountains called *favelas*, where the poor people lived. He explained to me that they had no police in that area and only the army could go in if any trouble came up. This *favelas* was a beautiful place filled with giant exotic plants, and the shacks looked neat and were colorful. An old lady with no teeth sold me a quarter of a kilo of grass for the $10 I had just made. She wrapped it up in a newspaper. I had two days to smoke it before going home.

Sitting down in my hotel room in Ipanema, I rolled a big fat joint and lit it. It burned my throat, and I coughed for a few minutes. *The next puff I will take in more air to cool my throat,* I thought. Four hours later, I was still sitting there in the same position. The stuff was just too strong for me, and I couldn't move at all. I gave it away to my friends and took the plane back to New York.

Paul and I didn't like each other. My last tour with him was in the Midwest. The gigs paid little, and the music was worse. He had a brand-new band for this tour, and I was the lone pothead. One morning, Paul barged into my motel room and demanded that I give him my stash so that he could flush it down the toilet. He threatened to fire me. When I refused, he said, "I'm charging you for the cost of a replacement," and grabbed my alto flute. I had to tackle him to take it back.

About half hour later, he dropped me off at the bus stop in Carbondale, Illinois. The bus stop reminded me of the scene from the movie *North by Northwest*, where Cary Grant gets attacked by a crop duster. Paul called my dad and told him that he had just fired me for being a pothead. I wonder if Dad was smoking when he got the call. The bus fare was $30, and I had about $35. Thus the most uncreative period in my life was over.

Shortly after I came home, I received an eviction notice. My landlord claimed that I was playing my flute too loud in my apartment. I got a lawyer, haircut and new suit, and went to court. The landlord's lawyer said to me, "I have only one question. Did you get a haircut because you're coming to court?" implying that I was, in fact, a long-haired hippie.

I looked to my lawyer for help, but he looked away from me, and I lost. I wasn't going to appeal, so I began looking for a new apartment. Greenwich Village had become popular, and rents had gone up. I found a place on Fifty-First Street between Eleventh and Twelfth Avenues, which was the only apartment building on that block. An old Jewish millionaire had kept it so he could have a view of the Hudson River. The view from my window was spectacular: the *Queen Elizabeth II* was on the right, and the *Michelangelo* on the left.

Since my accident in Bermuda, I had recovered my health, but I now needed to get my creativity back. I was a shadow of my old musical self. I needed to learn how to play the flute again. The mescaline trip with Jeep affected my ability to play creative music. *What if I take my mind to the place where I lost it?* I wondered. I read a book on LSD, a drug that's in the same category as mescaline and psilocybin. The author, Bernard Roseman, had figured out how to learn at an accelerated pace using methods he taught himself by studying the Tarahumaran peyote ceremonies. I got a sugar cube with acid in it and took a trip. I tried to draw, but the line came off the paper into the air, and I couldn't control it. All I could do was scribble like a little kid.

I studied the book more carefully. Roseman had taught himself how to type in two days. His method was to get totally involved in the problem at hand for a few days and then take LSD. When it hit, he stayed with his problem and did not quit, lie down, take his clothes off, and giggle, which is what most people end up doing on their trips. I used his method playing the flute during my trips in my apartment, and my musical brain began to return. It took a number of trips before I was playing well again. I also improved my drawing while in a psychedelic state.

I went back to the nightclubs in the Village and resumed sitting in. My favorite place was the Cafe Au Go Go on Bleecker Street. Each week, a new band came in to play, and many of them became famous. I sat in with Blood, Sweat & Tears, the Paul Butterfield Blues Band, and the James Cotton Blues Band. I also played with Junior Wells for a week.

One night, Junior announced to the audience that a real wild man was going to sit in with us—Jimi Hendrix. Jimi's style of playing began with the blues. He and Junior were a perfect match. I was swept away by the electricity of the moment; it felt beautiful. Nobody knew who Jimi was yet, but they knew that something special was happening. He even played a solo with his teeth.

He was a cosmic player, but off stage, he was very sweet and soft-spoken. I had first met him when he was a back-up guitarist for Jeep. He wore paisley shirts with big ruffled sleeves. He looked great in them, so I went out and got myself one. He told me about working with Little Richard. Jimi and the bass player went out one day and bought fancy shirts for the gig. After the gig was over, Little Richard came to Jimi's room and threw the gig money in his face and said, "Don't ever try to look better than Little Richard," and fired him.

I played with Jimi in a jam session at the Gaslight Cafe a tiny club on MacDougal Street. Bob Dylan did his first solo gig there. We also played a set as a duo at the club called the Scene on Forty-Seventh Street. Jimi plugged in his wah-wah pedal (a new invention at the time) and said, "I can't play without this."

It sounded as if his guitar was talking. At the time, I was tripping on mescaline, and playing this set was one of the greatest experiences I've ever had. That night he drove me home in his Corvette.

Jimi wasn't the only legendary figure to pass through Cafe Au Go Go. I had the opportunity to do a week with Big Joe Williams. He was an old blues singer with a seven-string guitar. We also did a radio show together. Joe was about seventy-five and would drink a pitcher of beer in between sets. I asked him if he had ever met Robert Johnson.

"Yes, I knew Robert," he said.

When we played opposite the Muddy Waters Blues Band, Muddy Waters pointed to Joe and said, "That's my teacher."

In the late '60s, I was making frequent trips up to WBAI, a listeners-sponsored radio station, from my apartment on Bedford Street. I had moved from the apartment on Fifty-First Street, where I lived for about a year, back to the Village. I'd call up Bob Fass, the DJ for a show called *Radio Unnameable*, and if he had a spot open, he'd say, "Come right up."

I'd smoke a joint, get in a cab, and be there in fifteen minutes. Bob credits me with giving him his first joint. He would let me play for hours, sometimes by myself. He would mix in all kinds of stuff with the flute: tapes of politicians making speeches, whales singing, comedians, and various sound effects. One time he poured water from one glass to another. Sometimes I would take other musicians with me to the station so they could get some publicity, and in return, I would be invited to a celebrity's party.

On one such occasion, I met Arthur Miller and played duets with the writer Frank Conroy, as well as the pianist Peter Duchin, at George Plimpton's house by the East River.

George said to me, "I hear you like to smoke," and shared some terrific weed with me.

Being a Villager was the in thing.

One day, I bumped into someone from my childhood—the friend of Walsh's from the fight on Fourth Street where I was stabbed.

"Hi," I said.

"You don't want to say hi to me," he said. "I'm the guy that stabbed you."

I told him that we were kids when that happened, and I didn't hold it against him. Then he said, "I listen to you on WBAI."

What a nice moment!

Some very cute girls donated their time to WBAI, and a lot of hanky-panky went on in the bathroom. One time I got hold of some great mescaline, took it, and went up to the station. I thought to myself, *No one is as loose and free as I am right now.* When I arrived at the station, Bob was having a nude-in—everybody was naked. Bob was engineering in his underpants. I then realized that I wasn't as free as I thought. Some of the men had terrible body odor. I certainly didn't have the nerve to get naked with them. I went home without playing. Bob, at the age of seventy-six years (in 2009), still has a show every Thursday night.

This was the height of the free love era. Sex was in the air. No need to make a date—just take a walk to the nearest coffee shop or nightclub, or just take a walk. Sometimes the doorbell would ring five to ten minutes after a woman left my apartment, and the whole process would begin again. Often, I would get with the wife or girlfriend of another musician I knew. This went on for the entire time I was living on Bedford Street, until I became thirty.

Bill Evans came to the Cafe Au Go Go, so I went backstage to say hello. It was great to see him again. I had not seen him since Daytona Beach. He asked me how my career was going. I told him that *Flute Fever* had been out for several years, but I hadn't gotten any work from it; Columbia didn't renew my contract after *Flute Fever*. Bill said that people were listening to my record in different parts of the country and that it would pay off eventually. That was a big lesson. He asked me to sit in with him, so I got up on the stage and saw John Hammond Sr. sitting in the first row, two feet away from me. Bill asked me to come back and play the last set for the whole engagement. That's when my luck and life began to change.

Four

JAZZ ROCK

The next week, Jim Hall joined Bill's trio, and I got to play with both Bill and Jim. The following two weeks, Tim Hardin came to the Cafe Au Go Go, and I played with him as a duo. Tim asked me to put a rhythm section together to play a week at the Scene. I called Warren Bernhardt. Donald MacDonald, who played drums, and Don Payne, who played bass, were part of the singing group Jackie and Roy across town at a club called L'Intrigue. I hired them to complete the group.

Our gig started out well. Tim wrote beautiful tunes, but he was strung out on heroin. He was shooting up in his knees. When he went up on stage, you could see the bloodstains on both knees of his pants. Two days into the week he disappeared, and the group had to finish the gig without him. We kept playing his songs all week. They sounded good on the flute, and I recorded some of them later on my album called *This Is Jeremy Steig*. The week after Tim's disappearance, I was offered a job at L'Intrigue. I had a nice group, but the singer was gone. I decided to fill Tim's spot with Adrian Guillery.

Adrian was an artist and musician. He wrote his own songs and sang the blues. I had met him through my dad. My father had noticed a very beautiful woman who would sit in Washington Square with her boyfriend, Dan Basin, an artist. He became acquainted with Dan, probably in an attempt to meet his girlfriend. One day, Dad called me from Dan's house and invited me over to meet him. That's when I met Adrian, who was a friend of Dan's. He and I began playing music together at his house and eventually got a gig at the Café Rafeo. The stage was by the door, and people in the street could hear and see us through a large glass front. Whenever people would pass by in my line of sight, I would play my hottest licks to draw them into the café—the best advertising is the music itself.

Rafeo owned the building, which had his café in it. He tried to evict an old man from one of the rooms in the building. The old man was a retired mafia hit man. He chased Rafeo across Bleecker Street and shot him. He died in the doorway of a liquor store.

Adrian was perfect for me. I met him a little after I had fried my brain with mescaline, and I had difficulty playing very good jazz with its more difficult changes and rhythms. Adrian and I played some basic stuff, but it felt good and people loved it.

One night, when I was working at the Scene with Adrian, Tiny Tim sat in with us. He had me announce him as Larry Love, one of his aliases. He was one of the strangest and sweetest people in the music business. I first saw him perform at the Fat Black Pussycat. I've never met anyone like him. He had long curly hair, a big nose, and went around town in an old overcoat. He collected sheet music, which he carried in shopping bags. He had a great knowledge of

twentieth-century songs and could play all the right changes on his ukulele. His voice had about a four-octave range. He had rich, beautiful low tones as well as a comical falsetto. Some people laughed at him, but he was extremely musical. He called me Mr. Jeremy. While talking with me, he would go back and forth between his two personas. On hearing my joke, he would laugh in his high girl's voice, and then he would go back to his distinguished low voice. I was a big fan.

My group from the L'Intrigue gig, to my knowledge, was the very first jazz rock group. It came about not out of a vision but from a bad mescaline trip, a strung-out songwriter who had disappeared, and a flute player who wanted to improvise no matter what kind of music he was playing. That gig was a big success. The jazz critic Whitney Balliett reviewed us in the *New Yorker*, and a guy named John Court approached me about management. John brought an old guy with him to meet with me. The old guy looked just like your classic flasher—he was fat; had long, messy gray hair; and was wearing a trench coat. That was his boss, Albert Grossman.

Albert handled all the big names, including Richie Havens, Bob Dylan, Odetta, and the Band. I signed a contract with John. The managers would receive a 35 percent commission if they could get a record deal in ninety days. They got my group a deal with Reprise Records. Thirty-five percent sounds reasonable until you do the math. First of all, when I asked them about work, I was told that managers didn't get gigs. They said that I would need an agent at another 15 percent. All expenses came out of the band's share, which was 50 percent. It included travel, hotels, food, the engineer, the five of us, roadies, and the plane fare for the producer and his girlfriend. Needless to say, I never made any money. The deal was a rotten one but the only way for me to get known.

We decided to call our first album *Jeremy & the Satyrs*, which was also the name of the band. I liked to draw satyrs and nymphs, and one of my drawings was used on the cover. I hired Eddie Gomez to play the bass. My first album, *Flute Fever,* was done in Columbia's biggest studio, which had only a four-track machine. Since then, the recording industry had expanded to eight. I did a little introduction to one of Adrian's tunes by overdubbing three flutes, and Adrian did some emotional singing on the record. We had our own sound.

The big difference between this album and *Flute Fever* was that we were put to work. The first gig we played under management was at Club 47 in Boston, which was filmed for the movie *Jeremy*. We also did a television show for Channel 2 while we were in Boston.

In New York, we played opposite Freddie Hubbard for a week at the Village Vanguard. I had a Barcus Berry pickup on my flute. It sounded awful, but it gave the flute enough volume to rock. When I wasn't taking a solo, I would draw. We hung a white sheet behind the band and set up an overhead projector behind it. The audience could see only the shadow of my hand, and the drawings came out in color. The bit was great, but the Vanguard was very dark, and my felt-tip markers were always falling on the floor and getting lost. We also had this filmed. The filmmaker was using all kinds of bright lights in the club, which made the owner, Max Gordon, angry. Max never hired me again. The memorable quote from that gig came from Freddie Hubbard: "We don't need no electricity to play the blues."

In March 1968, the Satyrs traveled to San Francisco to play at the Fillmore Auditorium. This gig was our biggest in the short while that the band stayed together. Joe Beck joined us on the electric bass. I flew in by myself. When I arrived at JFK, I was told that no tickets were listed under my name. I said, "That's impossible."

"The computer doesn't lie," said the lady at the counter.

I've never trusted computers since then. I was able to leave the next day and arrived in San Francisco just in time for the gig.

Our management didn't reserve hotel rooms for us. We had to make friends in San Francisco who would let us stay with them. The atmosphere was very friendly, and finding people to stay with was not so hard to do. I was too much of a hippie myself to realize that the management owed me a hotel room at least.

San Francisco reminded me of what had happened in the Village during my teenage years, except on a much larger scale and louder. Bands were playing in the parks with stacks of amplifiers. Music filled the air, though it wasn't jazz. But musicians were improvising. Everybody was wearing hippie clothing, such as tie-dye, bell-bottoms, and headbands. And of course, all the guys had long hair. I fit right in, though I was just saving money on my haircuts.

Everywhere I looked, people were smoking pot, and I was offered a hit many times, which I usually accepted. The world was becoming civilized, at least in San Francisco. The Vietnam War was going on, but the people I met there thought the war was a terrible mistake. The hippie culture of San Francisco was about love, not war. The hippie clothes and drugs were not shared by warmongers.

The first gig was opposite Cream. The auditorium seated three thousand people and was one of the largest places I had ever played. Backstage, we met the promoter, Bill Graham, who later wrote nice reviews about my playing in his book. I passed Cream's dressing room. They looked like three sitting statues in a room full of thick pot smoke. It didn't look like they were ready to receive us, so we never met.

Playing for three thousand people has its advantages. I had never performed in San Francisco, and my fan base, up to then, was mainly composed of jazz fans. But playing when that many people are eager to receive you is extremely easy. The audience also understood the jazz element of our band because rock at that time involved a great deal of improvisation. The word for those times was *freedom*. And freedom in music is improvisation.

The second gig was at Winterland. It held five thousand specta- tors and had about twenty people running a huge light show that covered an entire wall. Just about all five thousand concertgoers were smoking grass. The aroma was incredible. Blood, Sweat & Tears and the James Cotton Blues Band were also on the program. Cream knew how to play superloud and make it work. Their album *Wheels of Fire* was recorded during this gig.

We played a mixture of Adrian's songs, a few jazz standards, and free music. I played a flute solo for the intro to a tune called "(Let's Go to the) Movie Show." The light show was up behind me over my head, in which little devils danced across the wall. Five thousand heads were swaying back and forth. The flute is not usually associ- ated with rock, but I've always known that you could play anything on the instrument. My experiences of sitting in with musicians who played different types of music taught me that. To give rock 'n' roll power to the flute, I practically screamed into it while playing.

We had about three weeks between the first two gigs and the last. We stayed with our friends in the city and soaked up the atmosphere. I heard a lot of terrific bands play in venues larger than I had been used to in New York. On one occasion, Joe Beck sat in with the Grateful Dead in a huge club.

The last gig was at the Avalon Ballroom. Eddie Gomez flew out from New York to play the bass and had his first and perhaps last experience playing insanely loud. We plugged him into a Marshall amp and jacked his volume way up. Bill Graham was going to give us three more weeks at the Fillmore, which I would have loved. However, some members of my band got ugly with him over how many guests they could bring for free, and Bill changed his mind.

Before going home, I went to hear the group the Electric Flag at Winterland. My friend Mike Bloomfield was the guitarist. He invited me to sit in, and I enjoyed it immensely. On the way to the stage, people were giving me hits off their joints. This was the real rock deal for me. After the concert was over, many groupies lined up by the stage to be picked up by the band. I found a dealer on the floor and copped ten mescaline pills, one of which I gave to my father when I returned to New York. He had been experiencing a drawing block. In fact, he hadn't done a drawing that he liked for about a year. On the night of his mescaline trip, he illustrated the entire book entitled *CDB!* It became one of his best-selling children's books. Needless to say, the trip put an end to his drawing block.

I must say that my experiences in the month I was in San Francisco were more about being in the center of a huge spectacle than playing music. After my trip to the West Coast, I knew why rock stars were so full of themselves. If I'd had many more of those gigs, it might have ruined my personality permanently. Today when I play jazz, I'm aware only of the other musicians whom I'm playing with. It doesn't make any difference how many people are listening in the audience. The only thing that matters is the music.

Back in New York, we got a steady gig at the Dom on Saint Mark's Place. We worked there for two months until they fired us for showing up late too many times. I had no control over the band. I had something like a communist philosophy about my band, and I let the members know that I trusted them to contribute equally. Unfortunately, they took me too literally and decided to do whatever the hell they wanted to do. It included tardiness and nastiness to club owners, the audience, and each other.

One night, we played as loud as we had in San Francisco and shook the walls of the Dom with our volume. Half the crowd ran out covering their ears while the rest were in ecstasy. They had probably taken some too. Warren accused Adrian of trying to break his eardrums. He even went to the doctor the next day to get his ears checked.

At the Electric Circus upstairs from the Dom, we played opposite Frank Zappa's the Mothers of Invention. Frank said to me, "If you ever get tired of being a leader, you can be a Mother."

He must have sensed what a pain my band was to me.

"No thanks," I replied.

I'd seen how he made fun of the guys in his band on stage. I remember him putting a dildo on the high hat of the drums and then placing a doll on top of it. In vaudeville, spectators would sometimes throw tomatoes at a bad act, but Frank threw tomatoes at the audience. He was far too unpredictable for me to take a chance on being a Mother. Having said that, I still think he was a musical genius. I'm glad I had a few chances to sit in with him.

To me, the highlight of the Satyrs' experience was the time we played at the Cafe Au Go Go opposite Richie Havens. At the last minute, Jimi Hendrix, who had recently come back from England, was added to the bill. He had just become famous, and people were lined up around the block. My band opened the show. I remember that Adrian had a US Air Force jacket on, which had a dragon embroidered on it with the words "Death from Above."

The band members behaved themselves that night. The specialness of the event kept them from wanting to mess up the music. The audience loved us. They loved Richie. But when Jimi came out, the place exploded. I've never heard anyone with that kind of energy. I was watching from about twenty feet away. Jimi had told me that everyone expected him to destroy his guitars during his act. That night, he stuck his guitar neck through the low ceiling and made about ten holes in it. Richie and my band fed off Jimi's energy, and we sounded hot for the whole engagement. I wish I had recorded all of us.

The Satyrs came to an end without warning. When we worked for three days in Ann Arbor, Michigan, I quarreled with Adrian after the first night's gig. Adrian used to flip out about nothing. The next night, he stayed in his room and played his flute all night, so we played the gig without him. The next morning, he acted as if nothing had happened. I started to wonder if I really needed a singer.

My last project with Adrian was a soundtrack for a filmmaker, for whom we had worked before. The session was a disaster. The band had gotten hold of some peyote buttons, and all of us were tripping. Adrian lost his mind while we were recording. He kept playing a downward scale for eight consecutive hours. I'm not exaggerating. We begged him to stop, but he would just look up coldly and repeat the scale. He was put in an asylum on two different occasions, and the band broke up. He told me that he was a favorite patient there because of his music and art.

I didn't feel bad about the breakup of my band. The split was like a divorce from a bad marriage. In my heart, I really wanted to play jazz.

Unfortunately, the Satyrs had a problem with playing jazz tunes because Adrian had never done it before. The band was able to make it temporarily in the rock scene because we had a crazy enough singer who wrote catchy tunes. I was a good rock flute player, but the sound systems at the clubs in those days weren't advanced enough to give the flute the volume it needed. I could never hear myself on stage unless I screamed into the flute. Who knows what the audience was hearing.

Donald MacDonald was the Philly Joe Jones of jazz rock. He also played a mean samba. Warren was the only member of the band with an extensive musical education. I played by ear, and Adrian played from scratch. We never had a steady bass player. Don Payne, Eddie Gomez, Joe Beck, and Glen Moore all played with the band, but the Satyrs were really the four of us.

The band had tremendous energy, and people picked up on it. We were irresponsible, mostly from taking too many drugs, and I think that's why we didn't succeed. We also had no leadership. That was my fault. When our playing was on the same page, it was great, but at other times it was a train wreck. I remember the times we hung out, though. Adrian stayed overnight at Donald's house and painted three murals for him. He'd come over to my place, and we'd look at art books, play blues, and paint pictures together. Sometimes we'd do collaborations. That year was a unique time in history and my life, and I'll never forget it.

Five

PLAYING WITH BILL

was still young and began playing duo again with Eddie Gomez. I got an idea for a flute album. I would do side A as a duo with Eddie, while Paige Brook, my former flute teacher, would play classical on the other side. We recorded Paige playing Paul Hindemith and Francis Poulenc flute sonatas with an accompanying pianist. He was fantastic as usual. Eddie and I did the first recordings of our bass-flute duo. The concept was great, and the music was beautiful. If the record had come out I would have been proud to this day. Unfortunately, I had turned to John Court for the production. He said he couldn't sell it. I suspect that he didn't try too hard. This recording became another case of "the world not being ready," as my Aunt Margaret used to say.

Bill Evans began to work at the Village Gate on a regular basis. Eddie and Marty Morell had joined the trio. My apartment was only four blocks away from the club. I went to see Bill, and he invited me to sit in again. For the next ten years, I played the last set with him whenever he was in New York. Bill played three sets each night. I'd be there most of the night. These sessions were my jazz education. I'd listen to one or two sets of the trio, and then Bill would call me up on stage for the last set. We never talked about music. We just listened and played together. Bill wasn't known for playing free music. He always played his own compositions or standards. The two of us, however, would play free duos as introductions to some of the standards, which was very exciting for me.

In between sets, Eddie and Marty would come over to my apartment to relax and hang out. One night, I gave Marty a dose of LSD. In the next set, Bill quoted a line from "Santa Claus Is Comin' to Town" in his solo that goes, "You'd better watch out." Marty became paranoid. I had just met Ghost, who became a friend of mine and gave me free LSD. Ghost was a self-taught flute player. He lived in the East Village. I found him by accident through a friend. I often visited Ghost at his apartment and improvised with him. He liked my playing and began to provide me with acid free of charge, which I often took before sitting in with Bill.

One night, during a break, Bill introduced me to a goofy-looking black guy with a beard and glasses.

"This is Freddie the Freeloader," said Bill.

I instantly recognized his name as the title of one of Miles Davis's tunes. Freddie asked me if I could give him some money, and Bill laughed and said, "Now you know why they call him Freddie the Freeloader."

After almost every last set, Bill was out of the club before we could turn around. I read in a book that people called him the Phantom for doing this, but Eddie, Marty, and I called him the Lone Ranger. Sometimes Bill would go home early, and Eddie, Marty, and I would play trio, or Bill would ask another pianist in the audience to play the last set for him. Pianists were always in the audience checking Bill out. Among them were Warren Bernhardt, Jan Hammer, and Chick Corea. It seemed natural at the time to see all those important musicians along with many famous movie actors at the club. In those days, musicians were allowed into clubs for free. Today, you'd better have a hundred bucks to spend an evening at any club, which is the reason why musicians don't go to hear each other play any longer. Greenwich Village was the center of the creative universe. Musicians both rich and poor lived in Manhattan. Since then, everyone has moved out of the city for mortgaged three-story homes in New Jersey and elsewhere. I was one of the few that held on to their rent-stabilized apartments.

One night in 1969, Bill's trio and I played a particularly hot set. Afterward, Bill walked over to me and said, "We're recording with the quartet next week."

I had only one dose of acid. I took it for the first day of the recording, but we played for only two hours that day. Bill cut it short because he couldn't score his own dope. I stayed up all night tripping. I was a wreck the next day, and that's when we did most of the recording.

Having found his connection, Bill was in great shape for the recording. I remember him playing with his head hanging as low as the keyboard, and a long stream of drool went from his mouth to the floor—it was classic Bill. I didn't think I had played very well, but I've met a lot of flute players who said that they had taken up the flute after hearing the album, which was called *What's New*. Maybe it hadn't been as bad as I thought. Eddie Gomez called it "What's Old" because the material was a bunch of old standards. The studio where we recorded used to be a ballroom and later became a famous punk club called the Ritz. *What's New* was nominated for a Grammy, but we lost to Quincy Jones.

After the recording, the quartet became even hotter. We continued to play at the Gate. In the spring of 1969, the group played at the Newport Jazz Festival. We had to wait in the rain for eight hours before playing. Not knowing how long the wait was going to be, I took my dot as soon as I arrived, which resulted in using up a lot of energy prematurely. The stage was huge, and my microphone was about thirty feet away from the band. I had trouble hearing the tempo on the fast tunes, but "Lover Man" came out well.

I had a lot of other things happening in my life at that time. I got married again for two years and then divorced. I didn't have an agent or any kind of business sense, but the gigs just seemed to happen for me. I had a chance to play with Charles Mingus at a benefit at Fillmore East, the East Coast version of Bill Graham's Fillmore in San Francisco. The headliners were Mingus, David Amram, Norman Mailer, and myself. I had met Mingus in the early 1960s through my dad. Mingus's wife was a friend of my father's girlfriend back then. My dad, his girlfriend, and I went to Mingus's place for dinner. I was excited to meet him. I had listened to his band many times when Eric Dolphy was in it at the Showplace on Sixth Avenue and Fourth Street. At the dinner table, I asked Mingus whom he was using in his band. He motioned to everyone in the room—his wife and the three of us—and said, "This is my band."

He reminded me of my Aunt Margaret in a funny way.

Mingus once heard me play with Warren Bernhardt at a benefit and told me that he liked it. I was looking forward to playing with him. However, Mingus hired a bass player to play his part at Fillmore East. He had picked up a Latin electric bass for himself, which he fooled around with onstage for a little bit and put down. Then he put a candle on the stage to match the hippie atmosphere of Fillmore, and we began to play. When my turn came up to take a solo, Mingus came up to my microphone and made squeaking sounds by releasing air out of a balloon while I played. When the gig was over, I went up to him and said, "I've always wanted to play with you but not with the stupid balloon."

He looked really ashamed.

Since the Satyrs broke up, I had a different band for almost every gig. I was so stoned that the only reality was playing music. I signed a long contract with Sonny Lester without the aid of a lawyer. I didn't even try to negotiate for myself. The contract was for three albums a year at $1,000 apiece. It guaranteed that my playing would be out in the world—and that I would be poor. I hired Warren Bernhardt on piano, Donald MacDonald on drums, Sam Brown on guitar, and Glen Moore on bass for the first recording.

When we arrived at the studio, I gave Sam a dot, and we started to set up to record. Before I knew it, Sam was flat on his back. Glen bent over and put his ear to Sam's chest. Sam's heart was beating at a mile a minute. It turned out that he had done some smack, and it didn't mix well with the dot. The session was over that day. Sam recovered but not in time to be on the record.

Having stayed up all night on acid, I was exhausted the next day, but fortunately Warren gave me an ampoule of Methedrine. We recorded three of Tim Hardin's songs and completed the record in one session. The Methedrine kept me awake. When I listened to the record around 2004, I found that I had a terrible shaky sound. Oh, well. The album was called *This Is Jeremy Steig*.

After that album, I did two more records for United Artists: *Legwork* and *Wayfaring Stranger*. Sam played beautifully on both. He did, however, fall asleep on the second chorus of the title tune of the latter. When the second chorus was over, he woke up and played a third as if nothing had happened. That was my first splice: the engineer just snipped it out. The album won the Montreux Jazz Festival Grand Prix award for contemporary jazz recording. I was never invited to play the Festival.

Also in 1969, Sonny booked us in an all-star tour of Europe, which lasted ten days with a concert in a different country every night. How exciting! How exhausting! I got $600 for the whole gig, which included the money for a live record they were making of the tour. They paid for one meal and a continental breakfast each day. The word *continental* sounded fancy to me, but it turned out to be just bread and coffee.

The cast really was full of stars: the Thad Jones Mel Lewis Orchestra, Jimmy McGriff, Freddie Hubbard, and Kenny Burrell. I was playing trio with Ron Carter and Louis Hayes. The first night in Copenhagen, I went out with Thad Jones after the gig and jammed at a club. The musicians were incredible. They were older and played much better than I, but what the hell. I would be the mature musician someday, and the world would pass me by for younger ones.

The tour ended in London. Eddie Gomez and Marty Morell were playing with Bill Evans at Ronnie Scott's. Eddie and Marty picked me up at the hotel in one of those classic square English cabs. I played with Bill at the club that night.

Around this time, I received a call for a strange recording date. I was hired with two tabla players, Collin Walcott and Badal Roy, to play with some kind of a guru—a strange gig to play but that's what musicians have to do to survive. The gig could be for a wedding or funeral. Being a musician is not always a great way to make a living.

The whole studio was decorated with flowers. Rose petals were scattered on the floor. Just before we started to play, someone told us that the guru would be singing naked. He turned out to be a fat gay guy with a bleached Elvis haircut. He was no singer, but the three of us played our collective ass off. We made $200 apiece.

In 1970, Bill got a gig at the Berlin Jazz Days festival. This was even bigger than Fillmore. I was to leave for Berlin the day after everyone else. While I was packing, Eddie called me and said that Bill had been busted at the airport. He had two separate packs of dope with him. He managed to hide one in his suitcase, but they found the other in his jacket. The trio's trip to Germany was canceled. I was upset thinking about Bill's fate.

The Germans wanted me to come over and play with another band anyway, so I got ready to go. The festival had bought me a first-class plane ticket, but George Wein, the multimillionaire New York promoter, cashed in my ticket and replaced it with a cheap one to Luxemburg and pocketed the difference. How do I know that? Because George proudly told me so. I had to take five planes, and the trip took about twenty hours.

In Berlin, I played with some European guys—Daniel Humair from Switzerland played drums, Henri Texier from France played bass, and Gordon Beck from England played piano. The concert hall was huge, and the audience was in love with us. They clapped in unison and sounded like a giant metronome for five minutes after we finished playing. That's European enthusiasm. That never happens in the States. If Bill had been there that night, it would have probably been the biggest moment of my life as a jazz musician. But it turned out to be pretty special anyway.

When I returned to New York, Bill was out of jail and playing at Top of the Gate. I was afraid that the whole experience of being thrown in jail and not having access to drugs might do him in. He sensed my concerns and came over to talk to me at the club. He said that he was all right and told me the story about how he first got hooked. He was just snorting and thought he had it under control, until one day he found himself walking down his dealer's street. He didn't even know how he got there. He also told me that the heroin experience to him was "death through sleep."

Bill told me not to worry about him. He had been put on a methadone program. Heroin is always cut with all kinds of weird stuff, like baby laxative. Methadone is synthetic heroin, and since it is made legally, it is pure dope. Bill said that methadone got him much higher and didn't cost him anything. He was saving $600 a week. What hypocrites the dope treatment people are! They are no better than the pushers—both make money off the addict's habit.

Bill was actually in better shape than he had been before the festival in Berlin. And a lot of great music was yet to come. One night, I saw the difference: Bill didn't leave. Instead he went back to the piano after most of the people had left and played solo for a long time. We all stood around the piano and listened to something very special. Bill sounded like an orchestra.

He did a week at the Village Vanguard opposite Monk. To me, they are the two greatest jazz pianists in the history of the music. Even Miles Davis was in the audience. I heard just about every set that Bill and Monk played, and I joined Bill's trio for the last set.

At the end of the week, another miracle happened. After the gig was over, Monk sat down at the piano and played solo with the musicians standing around it—just like the time that we stood around listening to Bill. These two incidents happened within a few weeks of each other. Monk played a bunch of standards with his unique chord alterations. They were tunes I'd never heard on his solo records. I remember some great boogie-woogie bass lines. His music was magic.

The days when seasoned musicians would take the younger ones under their wings without being on a payroll are long gone. In those days, if you had the ears and talent, you could pick up all you needed simply by listening to them. Sitting in with Bill, I felt as if I was the luckiest guy in the world. To play and be friends with Bill was something you couldn't put a price on. More than forty years after the release of the LP *What's New*, here in Japan, people still bring almost pristine copies of it for me to sign the cover. Every once in a while I see Bill's autograph on them.

Six

ENERGY

had many opportunities to play a gig at a club called the Jazz Workshop in Boston. I usually stayed with my mother, who was teaching art at Lesley College. Sometimes staying there interfered with my sexual adventures, but these visits were the only times we could get together. She had a little mono cassette recorder that she used to record her classes. As soon as I saw it, I decided to see if it could record music at the club. I recorded the gig in which I played with Don Alias, who was on the conga, for the first time. After the gig was over, about twenty of us, including the band and musicians in town, packed into a room at the Lenox Hotel and listened to the tape. The Ghost had given me a piece of music paper with a tune written on it. The paper was also soaked in LSD. We all ate the music paper and flipped out over what we'd played. Every time after that, when I performed at the Jazz Workshop, someone would ask me if I had some more music.

The workshop was connected to Paul's Mall, which was an even bigger club. From the back door of the workshop, you could walk through a labyrinth of staff-only hallways and storage rooms. We used to smoke somewhere in the labyrinth. On one of these occasions, I lit a big joint and the great bassist Wilbur Ware appeared out of nowhere. Wilbur was a legend in jazz, but he was out of work because he couldn't control his heroin habit. He would go around to different clubs or stop musicians on the street and ask for five bucks. We all gave him money. He took the joint from my hand and finished it in one long drag. We stood there with our mouths open.

Aunt Margaret showed up at one of these gigs with an entourage of about forty graduate students. She had her own groupies. After my band had finished performing, I passed by two of the waitresses. They said, "We were just talking about the big event."

"Oh, you mean the great set we just played," I joked.

In fact, Margaret was giving her own standing-room-only lecture across the street. She filled up the concert hall three times and brought only her mouth and famous walking cane to the gig. Later, Joe Chambers, who was the drummer for that gig, told me that Alex Blake, our bassist, had asked him who Margaret Mead was. Joe explained to Alex how she went to New Guinea and lived with the headhunters.

Sonny Lester sold my contract to Capitol Records. He told me this shift was part of a $150,000 deal that involved me and two other artists. You see, when you sign with a producer, your price is fixed no matter how much he makes from a record deal. I would get my $1,000 a record forever. The vice president of Capitol wanted a rock 'n' roll record, and I tried to give it to him. I assembled a group with Don Alias on percussion; Jan Hammer, whom Don had recommended on a Fender Rhodes piano; David Spinoza on guitar; Jimmy Johnson on drums; and Jerry Jemmott on bass. All of them were exceptional studio musicians. We had a very commercial sound, but I think I tried too hard to please. When I went back to the vice president, he asked me if the music was rock. I told him to judge for himself. He didn't like it.

I put together a quartet with Jan, Don, and Gene Perla, and we went into Jimi Hendrix's Electric Lady Studios with no written music. We split an LSD dot four ways. I felt like I was flying a hundred feet above the flute player (me) and directing him by remote control. We called the takes "Rock No. 1," "Rock No. 2," and so on, except for the one called "Elephant Hump." We used Jimi's engineer, Eddie Kramer. In six hours, we had a record. When the vice president asked me if the album was rock, I said, "Oh, boy, is it *rock*."

I was very happy with the results and wanted it to come out. This time, the vice president liked it. We called the record *Energy*. I drew the cover. When we played some of it for Jimi, he loved it. He wanted to get together with the band after his trip to Europe. But he never made it back. I was at Electric Lady Studios when I first heard that he had died. Everyone in the studio watched the news on television and tried to make sense out of what had happened.

When the time came to record another album, Capitol told me that they already had it. Sonny had handed Capitol the outtakes, the unselected garbage from the *Energy* session. That infuriated me. What a cheap move! We had done only one six-hour session. I complained to Capitol, but they said that their expert had approved the new record. I complained some more, and they dropped me from the label. This put me out of work.

About a year later without a dime in my pocket, I was walking past the main Sam Goody store—the biggest record store in New York at the time—and saw the window filled up with about thirty copies of my new double album, *Fusion* (which was *Energy* along with the outtakes) on Sonny's own label, Groove Merchant. My face filled the window, and I didn't even have the money in my pocket to buy one. The photo of my face was from a commercial photo session that Sonny had arranged with Berry Berenson before the whole outtakes deception was revealed. Sonny never mentioned to me how he was going to use the photos. He was a crafty old fox. By the way, Berry the photographer was the wife of actor Anthony Perkins. She died in one of the planes that crashed into the World Trade Center in 2001.

Sonny refused to pay me for the new double album, so I called my lawyer. I finally became smart enough to get professional legal advice. He said we could sue Sonny for the $1,000 he owed me, but he was going to charge me the same amount for his services. Dad offered me the money, and I took him up on it. And thus I ended my relationship with Mr. Lester.

Jan Hammer joined John McLaughlin's Mahavishnu Orchestra. Don Alias went with Elvin Jones. And I met Tommy Bolin at Electric Lady Studios in a jam session. Tommy was a kid from Colorado who played great rock and blues guitar. He had the ability to fit right in with jazz musicians. His guitar playing was the closest thing to Jimi Hendrix in spirit and originality that I've ever heard.

For one of the gigs at Cafe Au Go Go, I hired Eddie and Marty from Bill Evan's trio. Tommy and his electric bassist Kenny Passarelli came from Colorado to complete the group. Tommy and Kenny stayed at my apartment on Bedford Street for the two weeks of the gig. Tommy didn't eat meat; he existed on spaghetti and salads. He was a big fan of James Taylor and Charlie "Bird" Parker. Tommy was about twenty, and this was his introduction to jazz. I loved the gig, but Tommy wasn't satisfied because he had to turn down his volume so Eddie's bass could be heard.

Tommy then invited me out to Colorado so I could be a rock 'n' roller for a month. I stayed at his house, and we played about ten concerts and a big club called Tulagi. This time Tommy cranked it up. He loved to press his guitar against his amplifier and play melodies with the resulting feedback, but he had to turn the volume all the way up to do it. People loved it. The audience could hear me, but sadly in those days the monitors on stage couldn't handle the flute, and I never heard a thing I was playing. I enjoyed playing with Tommy the most when we played acoustically at his house.

A few months later, Tommy came to New York again for a gig at Slugs', which we tried to record. He played so loud that my flute disappeared off the tape. Don Alias and Gene Perla were on the gig, but the tape was unusable—no flute. My bands were always drowning me out. Today's sound systems can accommodate the flute, but I came on the scene too soon.

Tommy went on to play with Deep Purple and then formed his own band, Energy. He told me that he stole the name from my record. When I saw him at the Bottom Line, his playing had gotten much stronger. I remember seeing a very pretty girl in the audience who was diddling off to Tommy's solo. I went backstage to see him, but he looked very unhealthy and unconnected. I sensed that I might never see him again. He told me again what he'd said many times before, which was that I was the guy that turned him on to jazz. I said, "Mention that in your next interview."

He did in a story for *Guitar* magazine.

Tommy died in 1976 at the age of twenty-five. I heard that he was on the road with his band and tried heroin for the first time. I wish I had told him about the girl I saw at the Bottom Line.

Seven

MORE PLAYING

Since my father divorced Kari, he had been living in an apartment on Washington Place, which was about five minutes on foot from my place on Bedford Street. I visited him often when I wasn't away. He almost made up for not having been around when I was growing up. He and I would smoke together. He said that it worked great with a drink. First, I was buying for him, but one day, he took me to his closet and showed me a large box with a pound of grass in it.

"I don't need your help in this matter anymore," he said.

While he was living there, he married Stephanie, who was a year older than I. She introduced him to amyl nitrite. My father said that it made sex very exciting. I was at their wedding—sort of. I was outside making out with his previous girlfriend in a Volkswagen. I saw the ceremony through the window. His marriage was over in two months.

In the late 1960s, Dad went to a party and met two women. He dated both. One of them was Jeanne, and she became his fourth wife. They decided to move to the country. My father grew two six-foot-high pot plants on his property in Connecticut. Then he suddenly quit smoking everything. He had also been a heavy cigarette smoker, and when he had gone from three packs to five a day, he realized that smoking that much was going to kill him.

When Dad moved out, I was able to get his apartment on Washington Place. Andy Smith, a friend of mine from the band in Bermuda, helped me move. He borrowed a truck loaded with lobster nets from a friend. We took them out and put them under the stairs in the hallway, packed up the truck with my furniture, and moved it up the street to Washington Place. When we returned to reclaim the lobster nets, they were gone. We ran over to Bleecker Street where all the fish stores were. We were lucky enough to find the nets at one of them. They had already been sold, but we were able to get them back.

I painted murals in the kitchen and the bathroom with Liquitex water-based paints. I painted trees going up to and over the ceiling in the kitchen and naked girls dancing in a flower field in the bathroom.

One night after a gig a bunch of musicians and artists came to my pad for an impromptu party. One of them was Allen Ginsberg. He quietly sat in the corner on the floor. This was before he shaved off his long messy hair and beard. Before leaving my apartment, he turned to me and said, "You should clean your house."

I lived in the same apartment for almost forty years, during which time it became a dumping ground for various friends and girlfriends. One night, Don Alias called me up and said that he needed a place to bring a girl. They went into my bedroom and stayed there all night. I was in the living room drawing. At one point, he brought her out completely naked, and she did a belly dance for me. He said, "I just wanted to blow your mind."

Then they went back into the bedroom.

Two days later, the belly dancer rang my doorbell. I let her in just as I had any other girl. This process continued every day until she had a key to my apartment. That was the beginning of our tumultuous fifteen-year on-and-off relationship.

Her family owned Blue Water Manor, which was the second largest resort on Lake George in upstate New York and open for ten weeks every summer. I spent too much time up there listening to my johnson instead of paying attention to my career. As they say, a stiff dick has no brains. Guys wanted her. She was a tall, exotic-looking Lithuanian with a great body. She spent four hours a day perfecting it at the Joffrey Ballet School. I put her in my band and let her belly dance at the end of each set—an even bigger mistake than signing with Sonny Lester. People in the music business were always trying to make me more commercial, and I wanted to do it without sacrificing my musical integrity. A half-naked dancer made sense to me. Improvising over belly dance music was easy with its odd time signatures and ethnic scales. I thought that adding visual entertainment would make me more commercial, but thinking that my audience needed to be distracted from what I was playing was a disastrous mistake. Many years later, Prince and Madonna used belly dancers on MTV. It's all about timing. When the Satyrs were formed, Albert Grossman said to me, "This stuff (jazz rock) is going to be big in a few years."

He was right, but my timing was off there as well.

My father hated the belly dancer (hereafter "Belly"). I brought her to the country twice. He and Jeanne would always have their dog lick off their plates after each meal. Belly made the mistake of telling them that this habit was unsanitary.

"Don't you know what kind of shit that dog's had his nose in all day?" she asked.

She was right, but nobody was allowed to correct the great cartoonist and his wife.

Belly's family had a friend who was a genuine psychic. Her name was Millie. Sometimes she saw dead American Indians standing by the lake where they had been living a few hundred years before. She was not your typical gypsy fortune-teller with a headband, rings, and beads. She was ordinary looking. She looked like a typical middle-aged country housewife who was on the heavy side. You would never guess in a million years how special she was.

One day, when I was at the resort, Millie came to visit. The resort handled about three hundred people a day. The dining room was jammed with people and was as big as the Bottom Line. While sitting in this incredibly noisy place, she gave me a short reading. Belly suggested that I ask her about my publishing, which I did. Millie said she saw a big mess, which it was (I was terrible at recordkeeping), and then she said, "I see a check made out to you for $5,000, but it's not yours."

A few days later, we set up a private reading. Before Millie came, I dropped some acid—big mistake. Millie felt it and said that I was too tense for her to see anything. She gave me some relaxing exercises, which helped a little. After that she was able to see only one thing: I had been a French soldier in the previous life and had been shot. That was it. I wonder what would have happened if I had not taken the LSD.

About a month later, a publishing check for $5,000 came in the mail. I thought about what Millie had said and called my lawyer to make sure that the money was mine. He said he would check it out and called me back the next day.

"The money's yours. The group Ten Years After recorded your tune 'Slow Blues in G,'" he said.

I spent the money. I guess I could have looked into it further. "Slow Blues in G" was an outtake from the Sonny Lester double album, and of course, it had no words. Ten Years After usually had vocals. Six months later, I received several letters from the American Society of Composers, Authors and Publishers demanding the money back. However, I had done the right thing in checking with the lawyer and I didn't have to repay it. Millie was right. The check wasn't mine.

In the early '70s, Joachim-Ernst Berendt, a German jazz critic, told me that a tour with a German band would give me an opportunity to return as a duo with Eddie Gomez. I took his advice and toured with a free music band called Association P.C. for a promoter named Volker Steppat. It was a bad match. The group couldn't play tunes or blues, so everything was made up. I thought that taking dots would help me find a way to turn what the band was doing into music, but most of the gigs were horrible. The only member I could play with was the pianist Joachim Kühn. He had a lot of technique but couldn't slow down. Every piece was a race to the finish line. Somehow the German crowds liked it, and I was invited back for another tour. I went with Belly. The first concert was in a large hall in Cologne. The first set went well, but the second opened with a belly dance. Behind the stage were about one hundred steps, which led to a little door at the top. When Belly stepped out of that door in her skimpy costume, a thousand Germans burst into uproarious laughter. They had come to hear jazz, and I think they considered belly dancing a strip show. Her dance was canceled for the rest of the tour.

Near the end of the tour, I played a flute summit in the Black Forest. Four flutists played: James Moody, Sahib Shihab, Chris Hinze, and myself. Each of us was required to bring an arrangement for four flutes. I had paid the guitarist Ralph Towner to write something for me. Chris brought a four-page extravaganza with mostly thirty-second notes.

James brought half a piece of manuscript paper with a blues melody on it. Sahib didn't bring anything.

I remember that in the end, all the prepared pieces were discarded. We played a blues piece, in which each of us took a long solo. Being deaf in the left ear, I had to have everybody else on my right, which made me the last person to take a solo. When my turn came, it didn't feel like anything else needed to be played. Unlike saxophone, flutes don't sound that different from each other. One good flute is enough. I should have worn an earplug in my good ear until my turn to play. Hindsight is twenty-twenty.

Belly wanted to go to Tunisia after the tour and bugged me quite a bit about it. After the gig was over, James Moody walked by us and whistled a line from Dizzy's "A Night in Tunisia." We never went.

My next tour was in Canada with John Abercrombie on guitar, David Earle Johnson on drums, and Chip Jackson on bass. Belly came along. Her performance was actually well received, especially in one club where many hookers would hang out. We even got a full-page review of the gig in the local paper, which was full of praise for me but really trashed Belly. It made her crazy, and she wouldn't let me keep the article. She created too much anxiety about her show, but I asked for it.

Larry Young was one of the greatest musicians I had the chance to play with in the early '70s. He was a space cadet like me. Larry loved to get as high as he could and make unforgettable music out of it. He was also hilarious and would always pick up my spirits.

I did four days with him at Slugs'. Half the gig was with Don Alias and the other half with Jimmy Molinari. Jimmy was a terrific drummer who dealt coke on the side. He had huge arms from lifting weights. I remember he thought I was crazy to ride my bike to the gig because the neighborhood was so dangerous. He was right. Jimmy was murdered over a bad dope deal. He was shot and thrown off his roof, which was across the street from Slugs'.

Larry decided to form his own band, a sextet, which I joined. I loved playing with him. We played an exciting gig at Max's Kansas City and then made a demo for Atlantic Records. We all took acid for it. I don't know what happened to the tapes. I would have loved to hear what we did. That was the last time I saw Larry before his untimely death.

In September 1972, I went to Munich to play a concert with Art Blakey. The concert was one of the events related to the Olympics. The Germans wanted Art to re-create the sound of his album *Orgy in Rhythm*. That made me Herbie Mann. The group was fabulous—four drummers and a rhythm section with George Cables on the piano and Stanley Clarke on bass. The drummers were Art, Tony Williams, and Buck Clarke with Ray Mantilla on congas. I had always loved Ray's playing since I heard him play with Herbie at the Village Gate when I was a teenager. I was thrilled to play in a band full of super-stars. I sewed two dots in my pants and got on the plane.

The gig in Munich went off without a hitch. The dot got rid of my jet lag, and I played with a lot of energy. After the concert, we went to a club where Art and I sat in and jammed. Art kept yelling, "Get mad," while we played.

We hit the road the next day and flew to Toulon, France. We played a concert that was held on a plateau with a cliff behind us. We were facing three thousand people. I took another dot, but the dot gods were not so good to me this time. Ray Mantilla's congas were right under my good ear, while the bass and piano were on my deaf one. All I could hear were drums. In other words, all the musical signals were on my deaf side. When I was not the leader, my request for a specific setup on the stage usually went unnoticed. Worse yet, the stage didn't have any monitors, and the wind was blowing at about thirty-five miles an hour right into my mouth. It drove me crazy.

Art never planned the sets, and lengthy drum battles carried on in between tunes. At one point, I thought they were playing George Cables's tune, and I started playing it. Then I realized they were playing one of mine. We were broadcasted all over Europe on television, and I felt like I had forgotten to put my pants on. When we were done with my tune, Art went to the microphone and said, "That was written *and arranged* by Jeremy Steig."

Tony Williams told a very interesting story when the whole band had dinner together. On one of his trips to Japan, he was busted after he tried to buy cigarette papers in the hotel lobby. He spent about ten days in jail there. When he returned to the United States, the FBI approached him. They wanted him to spy on his fellow musicians. Tony couldn't believe it. He refused. His story made me wonder which musicians had accepted the offer. The FBI doesn't even have to tap your phone. An informer becomes your friend, hangs out with you, and visits your home. Then one day, you see him testifying against you in court.

Whenever I made a trip abroad, no matter how beautiful my destination had been, I was always thrilled to be back at Washington Place in New York. But around that time, I began to think that my home was not the same place it used to be. I noticed that Washington Place was becoming a lot noisier and more dangerous. When I moved there, both sides of my apartment building were parking lots. I could see all the way up and down Sixth Avenue from my windows. However, this changed when the developers began to build expensive condos on both parking lots. I had to endure many months of pile drivers that continuously shook my apartment. The condos came with doormen to protect the tenants.

Around that time, crack moved into the Village, and criminals started mugging the people who lived in the buildings that didn't have a doorman. When I looked out the window, I could see crackheads all over the block smoking behind cars. They even came into the doorway of my building to smoke. My neighborhood reminded me of a Roach Motel with a visitor at every corner. I decided to leave my flute at home for the first time in my life. One week, two murders occurred in the Village, both a block away from me.

One night, not more than ten days after the murders, Belly and I came home late together. I saw a disheveled white man push the door open after we had entered. When we got to the elevator, I said to her, "Let's walk up the stairs."

"No, let's ride," she replied.

Getting on that elevator was like walking the plank. As soon as the doors closed, the man turned around and held a knife to my throat. His eyes were pinned. He made us empty every pocket on our clothes until we were cleaned out. He took about $200 and left. The next month, an old lady on the first floor was murdered. It took me about six months to get over my fear.

Everyone on the block, including me, started calling the cops on the drug addicts. Imagine that—me trying to get rid of the druggies. The police never came, even though people said that a lot of plain-clothed cops were on the street. The police officers didn't want to blow their cover. I'd see the crack dealers selling right outside the building, and I'd make a call: "Come now, and you'll catch them all." No one would show for half an hour. Let me be clear about this: I believe all drugs should be legal, as alcohol is, and people have the right to do what they want with their own bodies, but I was a prisoner in my own house, and that was too much to bear. It wasn't until four or five years later that the crackheads disappeared and moved to another part of the city.

The most upsetting noise came from the Mister Softee trucks that parked outside my window almost every day during the summer. The motor was never turned off and was so powerful that the walls of my apartment would vibrate. And of course, the trucks played the jingle. I missed hearing the folk singers playing the guitar in Washington Square Park. The coffeehouses were long gone too. Looking back, Tony William's story was a prelude to the changes that were to come, and New York was definitely changing.

My trips to Europe continued. Following the two strange tours with Association P.C., I toured Germany as a duo with Eddie Gomez. The duo from the bass room in Music and Art finally made it to Europe. We did a total of three tours in Germany. We played a two-hour concert almost every night of the week. They were the highlights of our long musical relationship that lasted forty years. When we were hot, Eddie could read my mind and I his. We played free music, but it had its own structure. The music wasn't free like in a free-for-all way; it had elements of bebop, classical, atonal, and funk.

On one of these duo tours, I brought my electronic equipment. I was able to create chords with the Echoplex. The fuzz tone made me sound something like an oboe. With the octave divider, I could be another bass. I had a box called a Mu-tron that gave the flute a great electronic attack. Eddie played his bass through a phaser. We were breaking new musical ground.

One night we played at a beautiful hall in Freiburg. During a moment of silence, some guy yelled out in a thick German accent, "Stop the foolish electronics."

Eddie calmly went up to the microphone and said, "If you have anything to say, write it on a piece of paper and give it to us after the concert."

When we finished playing, a line of people, mostly pretty girls, formed in front of me. My first thought was, *I'm going to get laid tonight.* Then I saw that they all had little pieces of paper with a question: Why are you attached to all those electronic devices?

At the end of the tour, we did a live recording in a concert hall in Bremen. At the sound check, I discovered that my Echoplex, which was a vital piece of equipment, was broken. We had to do the show acoustically. Eddie played a solo with his phaser, but that was it for the electronics. We thought that we had missed the opportunity for a new album because we felt that the electronic toys were essential to our music at that point.

We had cassette recordings from the previous gigs with the electronics and really loved one of them. We wanted to have it transferred to a higher quality professional tape, so we went to the hotel to get it. Just before the elevator door closed, the tape slipped out of my hands and fell through the door. The elevator descended to the first floor without the tape. We retrieved the tape, but we eventually decided to have an acoustic record and called it *Outlaws.*

Eddie, Marty Morell, and I had a trio that came from the nights when Bill would skip the last set at the Village Gate. In 1974, the three of us recorded *Monium*—a code word for dope, as in "You got any monium?" I fell in love with the chordless trio sound when I heard *Way Out West*—Sonny Rollins's record with Shelly Mann and Ray Brown. Without a piano or guitar, the harmonic improvising possibilities go way up.

The recording was originally for a German label that was supposed to pay for the studio in New York. But the check bounced, and I was left with a cassette of the recording and a bill to pay. So I reluctantly went to John Hammond Sr., who paid for the master tapes and gave us an extra session at Columbia.

The company asked me again to draw the cover, but somebody at the art department printed it on a piece of graph paper. I had made a simple line drawing of the band and Ray Mantilla, who joined us on one tune. The flute player was floating in the air. The art department enlarged it and made the rest of the band the size of crickets. They probably thought the cover needed more lines, which is the only reason I can think of to explain the grids of the graph paper. I was always having just as much trouble with the art departments as I was with the producers.

My most bizarre art department experience came with United Artists when I did an album entitled *Legwork*. The company and I had a mutual agreement that the art department would photograph me painting the naked legs of my third wife for the album cover. She wore a red minidress to the photo session. The photo studio was not equipped for painting, especially on a human being, but I obediently did what I was told. When I asked them why they weren't taking photos, they told me to finish the legs first. Let's face it—their idea for a record cover was pretty lame. The title *Legwork* would have made sense only if it had shown me actually painting. However, they took a picture of me playing the flute next to her.

I said to the head of the art department, who was present at the session, that I was unhappy about it. He took me to the corner of the room and told me a story. He once had to do a cover for one of their artists who made him follow him around for three days. He said that the guy had wasted his time. He then showed me the cover that he had created as the final product, which had a smear of ugly brown on it resembling something one didn't want to step in. What was I going to do? Thus, the album cover was printed with a photo of me playing the flute next to my then wife in a pair of colorful tights. I don't think anybody can tell by just looking at it that those legs had actually been painted.

When our jazz album *Monium* came out, jazz rock, which is currently called fusion, was finally beginning to make a profit. I went backward in time to playing a less commercial form of jazz—*Monium* didn't do well.

My new contract with Columbia was for another record in addition to *Monium*. The week before the record date, I still didn't have a band. That may sound impossible in today's environment, but back then finding excellent players in the neighborhood was not difficult. Also, my strength as a player was in improvising, and I've always felt that too much preparation took the spirit out of jazz. Columbia wasn't nice enough to pay the musicians for rehearsals either. That week, I bumped into Alphonse Mouzon at the Bottom Line. He said, "Why don't you give me one of those record dates?"

"Okay," I agreed. "How about next week?"

He introduced me to Anthony Jackson, a hot seventeen-year-old bass player. I also hired Ray Mantilla, Richie Beirach, and Johnny Winter, whom I had just met. Richie was a very talented pianist with great ears. He could hear all the chords that I was indicating in my free playing and was an excellent free player himself.

On the day of the recording, Johnny came down to New York in his Winnebago because no other transportation was available. The vehicle was parked outside Electric Lady Studios. In those days, I was hanging out at the belly dance clubs on Eighth Avenue and had written some tunes in that style for the recording. Alphonse Mouzon asked me about the belly dance flavor, and my belly dancer started to dance all over the studio to demonstrate. She actually danced during the recording without hitting any of the numerous expensive microphones. In hindsight, letting her do that was really stupid. Hammond Sr. never came to the date. He couldn't stand me, nor I him.

After the recording was finished, Johnny's manager told Columbia that they couldn't use Johnny's image on the cover. When that happened, Columbia's plans of using Johnny's presence to promote the record went up in smoke. They forgot that it was my record. We had the cover photo taken at the Egyptian Gardens, the most famous belly dance club in New York. All of us except for Johnny were there. Belly was decked out in her costume. Ray had a fez on. Alphonse was holding a gourd. I was wearing a blouse that belonged to Belly's grandmother and a black beret. We really didn't look like a jazz group.

To promote the record independently, I did a gig at the Bottom Line. Bruce Lundval, the new president of Columbia, sent three bottles of Dom Pérignon to our dressing room. I called the album *Temple of Birth.* Belly told me that belly dancers used to dance for women in labor to help them with their contractions. The title and cover ensured that nobody would buy it as a jazz record. If I was going to be ethnically influenced, I couldn't have made a worse choice. The United States had just begun hating the Arabs. I still find Arabian music incredibly funky and beautiful. It has odd time signatures, which encourage an interesting swing and a twenty-four-tone scale. They actually hear quarter tones. But if our government wants to write off one of the oldest and richest cultures in the world, they sure know how to do it—all the belly dance clubs on Eighth Avenue are long gone.

After *Temple of Birth*, Columbia picked up my contract option, which called for two albums for $10,000 apiece. On Monday after the gig at the Bottom Line, I called Hammond Sr. to ask when I was going to get my advance. My excitement did not last. He began to stutter, which was always a bad sign.

"W-w-w-we decided to g-g-give you y-y-your freedom."

I came right back at him, saying, "Okay, but the contract was picked up, and Columbia owes me $10,000."

"W-w-w-we're going to give you $600."

"You can't do that, I'll sue."

"You can sue Columbia, but I don't have to listen to you."

He hung up. That was the last contact I had with Hammond Sr. I went to my lawyer and told him my problem. He had negotiated the original contract, for which he had received about $2,000. He said, "Don't worry about it. I'll take care of things."

He went to Columbia and called me the very next day.

"Good news, Jem. (He picked up my nickname.) Let me explain. It would take three years to go to court, during which time you won't be able to record with anybody. It would also cost you about $3,000 to sue them. Instead, we've agreed to lop off three grand, and you get $7,000."

Minus his 10 percent, of course. My contracts with various record companies always had lucrative options, none of which were picked up. Generally speaking, options are not picked up. They are in the contract just in case an album has a rare hit. They are designed to entice musicians into making cheap records.

Tommy Bolin's ex-bassist Kenny Passarelli called and invited me to see his gig at Madison Square Garden. He was working with Elton John. The night before his concert, I went to meet the band in their hotel room. Elton wasn't there. I saw big lines of cocaine on the table, each of which was a foot and a half long.

Kenny had gotten me two excellent seats, so I took a girl who was a big Elton fan. He was a lot of fun to listen to. He put on a three-hour show and had a hot band and a synthesizer player who played some marvelous sound effects. Elton had a piano that was made to look like a jukebox. The most amazing part was all twenty thousand audience members sharing the same feelings together. The lights dimmed, and everyone lit matches. Elton played about three notes, and the whole place knew what song was coming up next. A swell of emotion went through the crowd. Tears came to my eyes. When twenty thousand people cry, you cry too. My date explained to me that this was a love song Bernie Taupin, Elton's lyricist, had written for his wife.

After Elton's concert, I took my date to the Village Vanguard, where I sat in with Bill. Marty Morell had left the group, and Philly Joe Jones was playing the drums along with Eddie Gomez. This band was a once-in-a-life-time dream. I remember playing Miles Davis's "All Blues." Philly Joe had the most swinging cymbal I've ever played with. After the gig, Philly Joe drove me around the corner to Washington Place, and we smoked a joint in his car. What a night that was!

About a year after *Temple of Birth*, I had my last Christmas dinner with Aunt Margaret. I wasn't crazy about her as a kid, but she mellowed and became a terrific old lady. She softened up to me after hearing me play at the Jazz Workshop in Boston. The dinner was with Liza, Lucy, her husband, Edi, and their daughter, Melinda, who couldn't have been more than six or seven at the time. Melinda had the misfortune of being born on Christmas Eve, so we usually celebrated her birthday instead of Christmas at my sister's. Before the dinner, Margaret set up a tiny chair and table facing the wall, brought Melinda a slice of cake and had her eat it facing the wall. When she was done, Margaret said, "Okay, your birthday's over. Merry Christmas, everyone."

That was the Aunt Margaret I grew up with.

I remember asking Margaret about cults like the Moonies. I thought she might have an interesting slant on the subject. She had no thoughts about the Moonies, but she didn't like the Scientologists, who she said were spying on people. Margaret also said that she was very disappointed with Jimmy Carter. She did not explain, but my guess is he didn't listen to her.

Before we left, I gave her a copy of *Temple of Birth* with its ethnic cover. Not to be outdone, Margaret gave me a double album of a talk between her and James Baldwin called *A Rap on Race.* I think she already had cancer, and this was good-bye. She died in 1978.

After Margaret's funeral, a memorial for her was held at the Museum of Natural History. The principal speaker was Barbara Walters. She was just as jive as I'd seen her on television. She recalled dropping Aunt Margaret off at her apartment on Central Park West. She said that Margaret seemed "so lonely." Typical Barbara Walters. What an insensitive comment for a memorial but, hey, these are the people who run the world.

I brought a quintet to a four-day gig at a club in Lakewood, New Jersey. The members were Jerry Jemmott on electric bass, Joe Chambers, Ray Mantilla, and Arthur Rhames, a young guitarist who was a legend in Bedford-Stuyvesant, Brooklyn. The five of us had to sleep in the attic of the club. The living conditions were extremely primitive, but the music was exciting.

Jerry was a great studio musician and played on just about everyone's record, including Aretha Franklin's. One night, he asked me how much time was left till the next set. I asked how much time he needed. He said, "I need about thirty minutes."

I thought he had eaten some bad food, but it turned out that he needed the time to chant. Jerry was a Buddhist. Being Buddhist was the in thing among wealthy studio guys. I heard from other musicians that studio guys would go to Richard Davis's townhouse once a week and chant for money. That was before synthesizers and drum machines took away most of the studio work. I'll bet you anything that a lot of them have given up chanting since the money dried up in the music business.

Arthur was constantly asking us questions about jazz. Joe had once played a tune with Coltrane, and Arthur wanted to know what Trane was like. Stuff like that. Meanwhile, we were busy picking up girls and partying. At the end of the gig, Arthur said to all of us, "I've been trying to learn about jazz from being around you guys, and all you talk about is dope and pussy."

Joe said, "Hell, that's what jazz is."

I couldn't have put it better myself. As I write this, athletes are being tested for a large variety of drugs through urine and blood samples. They must agree to give up their bodily fluids—their ultimate privacy—to get a medal. We are being spied on by our own computers. Everything we type into them stays and cannot be erased. Cameras are everywhere—on the street and in offices, stores, elevators, banks, and more—not to mention satellites. Cell phones are rigged so that your exact whereabouts are always known as long as you hold on to that phone. Cars are being hooked up to global tracking systems. George Orwell was right about the television watching everyone, but even his great mind couldn't conceive that everyone would be eagerly paying to be rid of individual privacy. In this kind of world, I wouldn't be surprised if the current situation with athletes extended to musicians and artists. In other words, what if a musician made a wonderful record and then failed a drug test? The result would be that the record would never be released, and the musician might go to prison. If this had been the situation in the heyday of jazz, there would be no Miles, Coltrane, Bill, or Bird records available.

The only real war going on is between people in power and everyone else.

As for the womanizing part of the jazz musicians' lives, that has already been suppressed because of STDs, especially AIDS. Going on the road used to be a joy for young musicians. Playing music was a spiritual experience. Jazz was very seductive music, and women were attracted to the musicians who played it. Ladies who would come back to the hotel with the musicians were not unusual. They felt that they knew us after listening to what we played just that night. People weren't afraid back then, and that made it possible for jazz musicians to enjoy life on the road. Jazz was a beautiful lifestyle.

In 1975, I hired Mike Nock on piano and Rick Laird on bass in addition to Joe and Ray for a six-week gig in Germany. We had a Mercedes Benz bus, two roadies, a driver, and a tour manager. I was finally on tour with my own jazz band. I was very excited about it. I took my electronic devices, and I wasn't confronted by my audience about them. Electronics had become more accepted. Joe and Ray had drum battles every night. During a break between the sets on one of the club dates in Wilhelmshaven, the band sat down at a table together. Rick turned to me and said, "Steig, your music sucks."

I didn't understand what he meant because everything we did in Germany was collective improvisation. He might as well have said, "I suck," since he was part of it. I don't use the expression "my music." All I've ever done as a leader is give them the freedom to express themselves.

Two days later, we played a large concert hall in Marburg. The audience gave us a standing ovation. As Rick stood there basking in glory (and probably feeling that the music didn't suck as much as he had thought), his electric bass slipped off his shoulder, hit the floor, and broke in half. He said that the accident was a message from his Guru telling him to quit playing music. I agreed with the content of the message, but I said, "No, your bass just fell off your shoulder," because I needed to finish the tour. Rick got hold of another bass and kept his mouth shut.

The tour ended up in Berlin. We had to drive through East Germany to get there. This was before the Berlin Wall came down. The West German guard demanded fifty marks to let us through his part of the border. He was a large robust fellow. We drove about fifty yards to the East German part of the border, where a skinny, meek East German guard said in a high-pitched voice, "Ten marks."

We laughed and gave him ten marks.

East Germany was bleak, to say the least. All I saw were tiny drab houses with small gardens in front. The trees were felled for fifty yards from the road so that no one could jump into a car and escape to West Germany. Every once in a while we saw a Soviet Army transport vehicle. The sky was gray. It rained most of the time in Germany. When we arrived in West Berlin, everything was lit up. Big colorful billboards and neon lights were everywhere. We played a terrific concert, which was recorded for the radio. I wish I had a copy.

On Halloween in 1976, I did a gig with Sam Brown in a joint called the Last Chance Salon in Albany. Anthony Jackson was playing the bass. When he asked to see the music we were going to play, I gave him a dot. Belly talked me into letting her do one last belly dance. Ghost, who was living in Albany at that time, showed up and sat in with me.

In the middle of the dance, about ten strange men with masks on suddenly surrounded Belly. One guy had a Nixon mask on. Another was dressed as a flasher, and he kept opening his raincoat to her. They formed a circle and danced around her. The whole situation was scary. For this particular dance, Belly had feathers taped to her fingertips. She started making screeching bird sounds at them. I was terrified that these people were actually the police about to bust the Ghost, but before we knew it, they were gone.

A year later, Ghost did get busted on the day after Halloween. He was busted for having the largest and most sophisticated LSD lab in American history. He had a computerized machine that dropped a hundred perfect doses on a piece of paper the size of a hundred-dollar bill. The Feds confiscated fifteen million doses. They were going to bust him on Halloween but decided that All Saints' Day was more fun. Four of the Feds went to the hospital when they tasted the acid as if it was heroin. You only need a hundred micrograms of acid to get blasted—a lick is an overdose.

Ghost asked Eddie Gomez and me to write letters to his parole officer saying that he was a promising jazz flute player, which we did. After nine months in jail, the Ghost went before the judge. As luck would have it, the judge's son had some problems that were alleviated in LSD therapy. Ghost was given ten years' probation. The acid spirits are powerful. Ghost said that his machine was on display at the Drug Enforcement Agency museum in Virginia. He was very proud of it. I'm going to see it someday.

GALLERY

Horns, c. 1960
Technical pen on paper, 19.0 × 27.8 cm (7.5 × 10.9 in)

1961
Technical pen on sketchbook leaf, 22.7 × 30.0 cm (8.9 × 11.8 in)

c. 1961
Technical pen on sketchbook leaf, 22.7 × 30.0 cm (8.9 × 11.8 in)

1979

Oil pastel on paper, 55.0 × 76.0 cm (21.7 × 29.9 in)

Photographed by Takashi Ito, Ito Photo Studio, Inc.

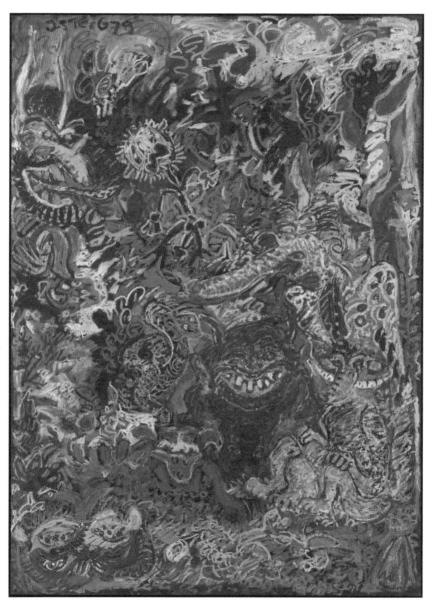

1979
Oil pastel on paper, 55.0 × 76.0 cm (21.7 × 29.9 in)
Photographed by Takashi Ito, Ito Photo Studio, Inc.

Sax Player Seduces, c. 2008
Acrylic ink on paper, 50.0 × 65.0 cm (19.7 × 25.6 in)
Photographed by Takashi Ito, Ito Photo Studio, Inc.

c. 2011
Acrylic ink and watercolor on paper, 25.1 × 33.2 cm (9.9 × 13.1 in)

2011
Acrylic ink, watercolor, and gel ink ballpoint pen on paper, 25.0 × 16.1 cm (9.8 × 6.3 in)

c. 2013

Acrylic ink, watercolor, and gel ink ballpoint pen on paper, 24.8 × 31.5 cm (9.8 × 12.4 in)

c. 2013

Acrylic ink and gel ink ballpoint pen on paper, 24.3 × 33.4 cm (9.6 × 13.1 in)

January 17, 2013
Acrylic ink, watercolor, water-soluble color pencil, and gel ink ballpoint pen on paper,
23.6 × 30.5 cm (9.3 × 12.0 in)

October 15, 2013
Acrylic ink on paper, 25.0 × 17.2 cm (9.8 × 6.8 in)

c. 2013
Acrylic ink and gel ink ballpoint pen on paper, 24.9 × 32.3 cm (9.8 × 12.7 in)

2014
Acrylic ink on paper, 24.8 × 32.1 cm (9.8 × 12.6 in)

2014
Acrylic ink on paper, 24.8 × 31.3 cm (9.8 x 12.3 in)

2014
Gel ink ballpoint pen on paper, 24.8 × 31.3 cm (9.8 × 12.3 in)

2015
Acrylic ink and watercolor on paper, 25.0 × 32.1 cm (9.8 × 12.6 in)

August 27, 2015
Acrylic ink and watercolor on paper, 32.5 × 49.5 cm (12.8 × 19.5 in)
Photographed by Takashi Ito, Ito Photo Studio, Inc.

2016
Acrylic ink and water-soluble color pencil on paper, 25.0 × 32.5 cm (9.8 × 12.8 in)

My Extracurricular Activity, 2011 and 2017

Paper cutouts created by Jeremy for the digital picture book Hananuruko *arranged on a sheet of colored paper by Asako to be exhibited at Jeremy's Gallery and Café*

Photographed by Takashi Ito, Ito Photo Studio, Inc.

Eight

ENDINGS

Back in New York, the quintet from the tour in Germany played a festival in Yonkers. That was the last time in the twentieth century I had my own group. The jazz scene was changing rapidly. Record producers coerced many top players to make commercial records. A trend had started and snowballed out of control. Jazz musicians were no longer in charge of their own music. Unfortunately, I, too, had to swallow my pride for money. I thought that I could make a commercial album and then go back to being who I was. But I was in over my head.

In 1977, I did an overdub on an Urbie Green album for the producer Creed Taylor. I took a solo singing into the flute, and Creed said I sounded like a wild animal. He told me if I'd do that all over a record, he would sign me to his label. I signed for ten thousand dollars for an album for the first year, followed by two albums for $10,000 apiece for the second year, and two more for $20,000 the year after that. The day after I signed, he called me and told me that I was to record the next day.

"I'm not prepared," I said.

"Don't worry about a thing. I'll get you together with Dave Matthews, our arranger, today, and you'll be ready tomorrow."

So I went. I showed Dave a few melody lines I had been fooling around with. The next day, he had them turned into neatly written charts for the band. Creed insisted on that day because Patti Austin had canceled out of her record date. The band had already been hired, and the studio had been paid for. He just didn't want to waste his money. Creed rhymes with "greed."

The band was terrific. Most of the guys from the band called Stuff were there. Steve Gadd was playing. He was and still is the hottest studio funk drummer. Eric Gale played the guitar and Richard Tee, the organ. Dave's charts were good. He's one of those guys who can go home with a sketch, write a big arrangement, take it to a copyist, and come back the next day and record it.

We did a six-hour date. Dave conducted, and I played in a sound booth. He kept on motioning me to keep playing. I couldn't believe it. I was doing a Creed Taylor record, and they were letting me play— it was too good to be true. I had heard some negative things about Creed, and I was doing it because I needed money. I didn't expect to have a good time. Of course, at that point, I didn't know how a Creed Taylor record was put together. And put together it was.

He said that they didn't get a good sound in the booth and that all the flute parts had been erased before I could even hear them. He told me I would have to do everything all over again. I was angry, but I had gone into the deal prepared for something like this.

When I came in to redo my flute, Hiram Bullock was overdubbing a singing guitar over what used to be my solo. The guitarist puts a tube in his mouth and mouths words as he plays—it's a guitar that talks. A good trick, but it had nothing to do with my approach to music. By the time they finished, I could hardly find a spot left for me to play on. I learned that Creed would always get someone else to star on his artists' records.

I decided I would get the star myself. I introduced him to Googie Coppola, an awesome singer and songwriter who could improvise but was also a religious nutcase. This made Creed happy. I was getting with the program. He was all set to make Googie a star. She had written a song called "Everything Is Coming to the Light," a nice song with great words, chords, and melody.

We prepared a track for her, but in the meantime, she signed a contract with Columbia. She decided she would never write such a great song again—a self-fulfilling prophecy—and wanted to do it on the Columbia record instead of doing it with me. Googie refused to sing her words on my record and went "Lu, lu, lu, lu" the whole song. The song was a disaster.

According to her husband, her album for Columbia was an expensive flop costing almost $300,000. Googie's producer went way over Googie's budget, obliterating her voice with more overdubs than even Creed had ever used.

Googie and I were to be featured improvising on another tune on my record. Before the recording began, Dave and Creed told me to play long tones and let Googie sing freely. When the record was completed, Googie was not on the track. When I asked what had happened, Dave and Creed said in unison, "It's *your* record."

That's how they got you to do what they wanted. I played "too many notes" for their tastes, so they tricked me into playing a solo of long tones.

We did a Bo Diddley beat on another tune. I screamed like a wild animal, and Creed was happy. Then he became Greed again. He gave me an old basic track that no one had been able to fix. Two or three bassists had already tried fixing it with overdubs. It really sucked. I refused to play on it and suggested that we finish the album with a Joe Chambers tune called "Hopscotch."

"Okay, but you can't use Joe on drums," Creed said.

Luckily Steve Gadd was also a great drummer, and the tune came out nice. At the overdub session, Creed made me play what seemed like fifty solos until I was tired and played "fewer notes." He had a lot of controlling tricks. "Hopscotch" was used for radio broadcasting to represent the album. A critic in *DownBeat* wrote that Creed knew how to make me sound better than I was—unbelievable.

I wonder why so many young people want to be in the music business when it's filled with controlling people who have no respect for music. I was told that this record, which was called *Firefly*, sold seventy thousand copies. However, it also killed my business in Germany. I was labeled a sellout. Germany didn't want me back. I was only invited back a few more times under very bad conditions with very little money.

The most important thing in the music business—aside from retaining your musical integrity—is to make sure that you get paid.

In 2004, the doorbell rang at my apartment in New York. My wife answered the door and found a tall guy with a German accent standing there asking to see me. He wanted to come in, but my wife told him to wait and came back to the living room to get me. The man was Volker Steppat, the German agent who booked my duo tour with Joe Chambers in 1978.

At the door, I asked him if he had come to pay me the $5,000 he still owed me from that tour. He said that he had paid off all his creditors except me and that I was the last one to get paid. I gave him my card so he could send me the money. He acted as if we were old friends. As soon as he left, my wife said that we would never hear from him again, and we haven't.

The 1978 duo tour was put together quickly, and Volker had only one-way tickets for Joe and me. After the tour was over, Volker said that he was waiting to get paid, and we had to stay in a hotel in Bremen for ten days. While waiting, I received a call from Eckart Rahn, a publisher I had met in New York. Somehow Eckart knew what was going on with us in Germany and said he could get us a record date so that we could make enough money to buy our own tickets back home.

The next time I saw Volker, he said that he had managed to dig up half of what he owed us. I had hired Joe, so I made sure that he was paid. I have not been paid yet to this day. Joe and I had to sneak out of the hotel in Bremen because Volker couldn't pay for our rooms.

We took a train to Cologne. Eddie Gomez flew from New York to do the album with us for Creative Music Productions, Kurt Renker's label. We got $2,000 apiece, and I was able to buy a ticket home. I had to give up my publishing royalties to Eckart as his fee for hooking me up with CMP.

For years, I would get statements that indicated my publishing royalties were less than $50 and he didn't have to write me a check if the money is less than fifty. This is not unusual in the music business, but the situation could have been avoided if I had insisted on a round-trip ticket. The CMP album was entitled *Lend Me Your Ears*.

In 1977, the winter was unbelievably cold in New York: the outside temperature was two degrees Fahrenheit. A girl I knew in Brazil named Claudia phoned me and said, "Come down and lie in the sun."

I couldn't resist. I loved Brazil from the Paul Winter tour, and the only thing that was missing last time was money. Now I had $10,000, and I wanted to turn the recent nonmusical recording experience with Creed Taylor into something good. I flew down to Rio that week. Claudia and I climbed Corcovado all the way up to the giant statue, which can be seen from anywhere in Rio.

Claudia was out in the daytime for her modeling jobs. I was stuck at the big house she was house-sitting for some rich people. I wrote some music. I wanted to play music but struggled to find musicians. Claudia said she could find work for me. About a week later, she took me to an agent named Gabby. Gabby got me a gig in a group with Victor Assis Brasil, an alto player. Victor was a terrible alcoholic. We played three concerts at a packed museum in Rio and a concert hall in Vitoria. I got $100 for each concert.

Gabby said all the other gigs were canceled except a big one at a place called Sugarloaf. This concert was also for $100, but I would have to wait over three weeks. I told her that I wasn't interested. I had brought plenty of money with me, and from then on I wanted to be on vacation. Besides, Victor had a terrible habit of jumping in on my solo and playing over it—something like the shows on Fox where guest commentators get interrupted. It angered Gabby that I wouldn't do the concert. She said that she'd make sure I would never work in Brazil again. No great loss.

I had been told not to drink the water in Brazil, but I loved the fruit drinks and thought they were safe. Not so. The ice was contaminated. I had incredible diarrhea. A doctor came to see me and prescribed a vitamin shot. In Brazil, you go to the drug store and get one right there. Claudia took me to the drug store, where a kid, who couldn't have been more than thirteen, came out with a needle. He soaked a cotton ball with alcohol, dabbed my arm, and gave me a shot. I was too weak to resist. Then he dropped the cotton ball on the dirty floor, picked it up, and tried to put it on my arm again. Claudia stopped him.

I lost twenty pounds and went down to 130—and I was skinny at 150. I bought some hip Brazilian clothes that fit skinny me, but after I gained my weight back in the States, they were like baby clothes.

I kept looking for people to play with for fun. Brazil is famous for its percussionists. I was told that Naná Vasconcelos was the best, but he had split for New York. Claudia and I went to Búzios, one of the most beautiful beaches in the world. The temperature was about eighty degrees Fahrenheit. We were there in December, and the beach was empty. The sand showed no footprints.

Six weeks later, we weren't getting along as well, and I flew back to New York. Belly picked me up at the airport. She had pink hair. As soon as I came home to New York, I got a record date with a Brazilian singer. Naná was the percussionist—a total coincidence.

After Eddie Gomez left the Bill Evans trio in 1978, I went down to the Vanguard to sit in again. That time, Bill seemed cold toward me and said he had to work things out with his new band. I think that Bill thought Eddie had left him to play with me. The truth was that Eddie went to play with the group called Steps (later renamed Steps Ahead). I don't think that Bill played in New York again until his very last gig.

In 1979, Eddie and I drove to a club date in Philadelphia. On the way, we heard on the car radio that an accident had occurred at the Three Mile Island nuclear plant. We were pretty close to the plant. As I played that night, I wondered if I had become radioactive. No one in the club seemed to know or care what had happened. The accident was big news for a few days, and the story disappeared.

A while later, Eddie and I did a benefit against nuclear energy in a church in the Village. We were the only band in the event. About one hundred people came. Most of the earlier benefits I had played were much larger in scale. But going into the '80s, large benefits tended to be played exclusively by superstars and for less controversial causes. War and nuclear energy were off the table.

One night, a taxi went through a red light, smashed into my bicycle, and sent me flying about forty feet. I landed on my hands and knees in the street by the Cooper Union art school. I tried to get up, and a voice told me to stay where I was. Unlike the accident in Bermuda, I didn't black out. The hit was so powerful that I thought I would surely die. As I lay there, I groaned, "It was my fault," because I didn't want anyone to go to jail for killing me.

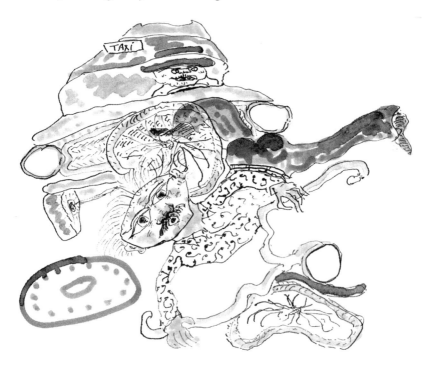

I suddenly began to worry about my flute. I had it on the handlebars of my bike. Luckily someone put it under my head. An ambulance took me to Bellevue Hospital. They took X-rays, but I didn't get admitted until five hours later. They put me in a chair where I sat in incredible pain.

Once in the room, I was on my back for fourteen hours and was given no food, water, or painkillers. At the end of the fourteen hours, an intern leaned over and told me to move my neck. I told him that I thought it was broken and that I didn't want to move it. He said, "Nonsense," and grabbed my head between his palms and forced it from one side to the other, causing me unbelievable pain. Then he left. I kept yelling out for help. I needed a painkiller, but no one came. Another guy in the room was also in a lot of pain and was moaning. He asked me what my problem was, and I told him. Then I asked what had happened to him, and he said, "I was shot."

The next day, just before two in the afternoon, I was given a strong painkiller. Visiting hours had also begun. I don't know how anybody found out where I was, but my father, Eddie Gomez, his son, Scott, and my dealer came to see me. This was the second life-threatening accident I had, but my mother was not immediately notified this time either.

My father began to talk about what interesting shadows the venetian blinds were making in my room. This somehow rubbed my dealer the wrong way, and the next time he saw me, he said that he thought my father was being extremely insensitive, talking about something like that after I had almost died. When the hospital said that my X-rays were negative for any breaks or fractures, my father rented an ambulance to take me home.

The next two weeks were hell. My head felt like it might fall off. When I got out of bed, I had to literally hold it with both hands. Belly came over and fed me. Someone gave me a doctor's name, and I went to see him. He booked me into Lenox Hill Hospital right away. When I arrived, I suggested that they check my X-rays.

"No, we'll take our own," the doctor said, but I was put in traction first.

Five days later, they took X-rays. Then an hour after that, four doctors ran into my room and moved me out of traction real fast. I had a broken neck. My hangman's bone (second cervical vertebrae) was broken. I was lucky to be alive, and the hospital was also lucky for not killing me by pulling my neck apart with traction. The doctor gave me a neck brace, which I was told to wear for six months. I split this place as fast as I had Bellevue and went home to recover.

I stayed in bed, drew, and wrote music. I was able to get $20,000 in compensation from the cab company. Being an independent musician, I didn't have health insurance. I went back to the hospital about six months later for a treatment that used some electronic device, which didn't help at all.

Belly moved back in with me. She told Millie the medium about my accident. Millie commented that I had just missed dying from it and that I should never attempt operating another vehicle of any kind because it would kill me. I've taken her advice. To this day, I don't have a driver's license.

A year later, I was able to function again, but I was already forgotten. Steady streams of phone calls and offers of gigs never resumed. When I had the accident, I had nobody advertising that I had been in a pretty serious one or that I was not able to play for months. However, people found out anyway. I didn't get any business propositions during the time I was home recuperating. Time had passed me by. I had no more work. Within a year, I became a has-been in the jazz scene.

Belly announced that she was going to form her own punk band, in which she would sing her own tunes and that I could play with her if I wanted to. I was dumb enough to accept that offer. She had her own money, so she paid for her gigs herself. She named the band The Tribe. I selected the band members, and we had a pretty hot band except for Belly. The personnel kept changing, but we always had good players. We hired Marvin Horn and later Bill Washer on guitar. Sabir Kamal was on drums. I think even Joe Chambers worked with us once. Belly hired Googie to be her backup singer, and Googie's husband, Tom Coppola, played keyboards. I found it funny that Googie was backing up Belly. Googie was one of my favorite singers, and Belly was mediocre at best. In fact, the band might have made it if Belly wasn't there. The punk club owners thought they were getting a Steig band and didn't like it when they found out that I was indeed a sideman in a circus.

Belly looked like an exotic bird with her multicolored hair and feathers attached to her fingertips. She wore extremely revealing tight leotards. The clubs would advertise the gig as mine, which made my fans angry. I would perform two of my own tunes first before the bird came prancing out. Once she hit the stage, I directed the band from the side. In a way, these shows were the closest I came to leading a band, except the singer and the material weren't happening. The bird had a big black light box built for the show, and we all wore clothes that glowed in the dark when the lights were off. The punk clubs in New York City never paid enough, but the bird made up the difference with her own money.

In 1980, Bill Evans died in the middle of his week in New York. I didn't go to hear him because people were saying that he was very sick, and I didn't want to see him that way. A big memorial was held for him at Saint Peter's Church in New York City. I played "Nardis," a tune I used to play with Bill, with Eddie, Warren Bernhardt, and Al Foster. I remember playing an angry solo. We lost Bill way too soon.

After the memorial, Bill's second wife asked me out to have a drink with some people. I didn't know any of them. At the table, she passed around an enlarged glossy close-up photo of Bill playing his last set before death. His face was full of pain. I found this inappropriate, but it seemed to give her pleasure. It brought to my mind a scene in the Village Vanguard from a few years earlier when she showed me a huge plastic key chain Bill had given her that had just the word *bitch* in capitals.

After passing around the photo, she took out a cassette. "Let's listen to Bill's last set," she said with glee. I left immediately. Being out with them all was very depressing.

I played with Bill for only one reason—for the joy of playing with him. Recently in 2011, I was contacted by a label that was going to put out a double album of Bill's trio at the Village Gate. They offered me $500 to write something for the album because I was part of the Village Gate experience. I refused.

To this day, people still put on many Bill Evans tribute concerts, and some are trying to make documentaries about him. I got to know some of the people involved in those Bill projects, but they didn't know that I played almost every night with Bill when he was in New York. Now I'm glad that my experience remains personal.

One of the documentary filmmakers delivered a letter to me from Bill's girlfriend from his last years. Along with the letter was a cartoon by Bill. She thanked me for "being such a good friend to Bill." I never met her in person, but it made me feel good to know that Bill remembered me that way.

In the 1980s, cocaine became the drug of choice for jazz musicians. I was a witness. Suddenly, coke was as available as ice cream. The musicians I knew shared the same connection. He was the son of a rabbi and a Republican. The customer couldn't simply go to his place, score, and leave. He or she'd have to hang out with him and sample his product, which always turned out to be far superior to what he'd sell. The connection would talk about topics that I wasn't particularly interested in, such as how he loved Ronald Reagan.

Sometimes drugs can be helpful, as in my father's case when he drew *CDB!* on mescaline, but cocaine is different. It's like cigarettes: the high is in the taking of the drug. I read that scientists experimented with monkeys. If you give a monkey a choice between cocaine and food it will keep taking the cocaine until it dies.

Coke destroys the nose, since it is sniffed and causes insomnia. People get nasty when they take it. It messes with men's ability to have an erection, while at the same time it makes people really horny. What a dreadful combination! It makes people horny and unable to perform sex and that makes them get even nastier. The transformation of music seemed to happen overnight. Musicians began to play too fast, leaving little warmth in the music.

The jazz club Bradley's on University Place in the Village was a perfect example of the jazz coke scene at that time. Bradley was a big scary-looking guy who resembled Lurch from the television show *The Addams Family*. He was actually a nice guy and loved jazz. When Paul Desmond died, he left his grand piano to Bradley's, and many great pianists got to play on it. Ninety-five percent of the crowd and musicians there did coke. In the bathroom, an exchange of one and ones, a sniff for each nostril usually occurred. I didn't particularly like the high that I got from coke, but just about everybody I liked to play with did it. They were afraid to hang out with those who didn't. It helped to be able to share toots in the bathroom.

New York City's cabaret law allowed only string instruments, including piano, to be played in an unlicensed club like Bradley's. Pianists and bassists continued to have steady work in the many duo houses that sprang up in the '80s. Horn players, however, could play only in licensed clubs, basically because horns were considered louder than string instruments—the same was true for drummers. Bradley was a good friend, but he couldn't hire me. He did allow me to sit in, which I did often. My work was drying up, and I needed to keep my chops in shape.

I had one memorable night at Bradley's. While I was playing a solo, a huge rat came out of the kitchen and ran through my feet. David Earle Johnson, who was playing the congas, picked it up by the tail and tossed it at Jan Hammer. Jan jumped straight in the air like Betty Boop in a cartoon. The customers screamed, and the place emptied. Bradley calmly walked over, swept the rat into the kitchen with a broom, and stomped it to death. He came out and said, "That was just a mouse. Why are you so afraid of a little mouse?"

Bradley's closed in 1996 supposedly because the bathroom wasn't built to handle wheelchairs, they said. I don't know if that was the real reason, but the rumor was that installing a new bathroom with a ramp would cost tens of thousands of dollars.

In 1983, I received a postcard about an art show that a friend was in. Liza had been staying with me at Washington Place. She had cancer and had left Boston. She was about to go into the hospital for the last time. I took her to the show, which was in a crowded, noisy disco. She said that she loved it. My older sister, Lucy, screamed at me for having taken Liza there, but that show was the last exciting life experience my mother had.

Liza kept her sense of humor until the end. On one of her last stays in the hospital, she let out a big fart in bed, and a beautiful, satisfying smile formed on her face.

The hospital looked down on the East River. Shortly before she passed away, the Fourth of July fireworks were held. They were shot off barges on the river. Liza was already in a coma, and I sat in the dark room with the flashes coming through the windows.

The day she died, she had an oxygen mask on. I saw her take her last breath. I didn't feel like hugging her body. She wasn't in it anymore. The weather was beautiful that day, and I thought that it was a good time for her to go to the next place. Neither Liza nor I are religious, but I felt that her soul was headed somewhere.

Lucy organized a memorial. She contacted Liza's friends and got hold of a lot of her oil and watercolor paintings to decorate the wall at the memorial. She put together a great art show. Liza had never tried to make it professionally as a painter. She gave her works to her friends, but her paintings belonged in a museum. She had many friends, and they stayed friends with her for her whole life. They all came to the memorial, but my father didn't show. Uncle Arthur read a poem that he had written for the occasion.

At the party
On first meeting
What took the eye

Was her attire
Of flapper and belle époque
In happy array. . . .

When she painted, her abandon
Was watched over
By angels of intuition.

Two weeks after Liza's death, I went to the country to see my dad. I thought it might cheer me up. I stayed for a few days. While talking about nothing in particular my father suddenly said to me, "I didn't love your mother. We never should have been together."

In my family, Dad was famous for his lack of tact. I wondered if he meant I was a mistake also but quickly put it out of my mind. That was the first time he said anything like that about Liza. In fact, he used to tell me how decent she was for not asking for child support.

Eddie Gomez and I sometimes got together at my apartment to jam. We did the master recording of the soundtrack for one of my father's books called *The Amazing Bone*, which is a story about a female pig that finds a talking bone. Most of my father's stories had sexual overtones, some of which he would explain to me. For example, the flower blooming in *The Zabajaba Jungle* with the hero in it represented an erection. In the case of *The Amazing Bone*, the bone was broken in half and looked very much like a dildo.

The recording was done in a studio in Connecticut. We played while listening to a voice track of the actor John Lithgow. He was terrific. As in the case of most overdubs, I never met him.

I did my first professional recording of my bottle drums for the movie. I taped empty bottles together and percussively tongued them on the top, a technique I had developed at home with my four-track tape recorder.

The music was beautiful, but the mixing was bad. Eddie Gomez and I paid for a remix out of our own pockets and hired James Farber. He is an excellent engineer, and *The Amazing Bone* stands out as a highlight in the life of the duo.

I also did the music for *Sylvester and the Magic Pebble* by my father, which was also narrated by John Lithgow. I wrote the music and hired Eddie and Dan Wall.

When I was not playing with Eddie, I found myself playing weddings. Sometimes I had to read classical pieces. A few times I had to play by myself in a tuxedo with crowds of drunken guests bumping into me with drinks in hand.

My crazy relationship with the belly-dancing bird ended after about fifteen years. One night while she was at her mother's she phoned me and said that she had a new boyfriend and she was serious about him. A week later, she called me from her honeymoon somewhere on a tropical island—she just wanted to let me know. A few days after the call, she came back and stayed with me for a week. She slept in the backroom of my apartment most of the time.

A while later, just before my next wife-to-be moved in, Belly came over to collect the rest of her things, and all hell broke loose. I looked around, and all I could see were my flutes out of their cases and a very expensive Neumann microphone. I had to get her out of my apartment before she broke something. I ran down the hallway while she kept drubbing me on the head. Once she was outside the door, I kicked her in the shins and locked the door. I never saw her again.

My face swelled up and I couldn't swallow, so I stopped eating. I became very sick. I would wake up in the morning and go back to sleep for another eight hours. I tried to play the flute, but it made my head feel as if it was being ripped apart to make the flute embouchure.

I found a Chinese doctor named Kenny Gong. Kenny was a doctor during the day and a martial arts teacher at night. He could break your arm or heal it. He was said to be the best doctor in Chinatown. When he examined me, he had a serious look on his face and gave me a bunch of powerful herbs. I began to feel better after a couple of treatments. The swelling went down in my face, and the headaches subsided. He told me later that he was afraid I would die and almost decided not to treat me. He didn't want anyone to die on him and often rejected patients. He said my heart had been skipping beats.

He told me that he could also try some acupuncture on my facial paralysis. The muscles under my left eye were weak and sagging from the accident in Bermuda. In the first treatment, Sifu, as everyone called him, inserted a needle into one of my toes. It hurt so much. Then he held up a mirror to my face to show that my left eye looked normal. This happened twenty-five years after the accident. I wrote a tune for him called "Sifu's Song."

I got married for the fourth time to a piano player. I brought her up to meet my dad in Connecticut. He had just finished a book called *Shrek!*, which means "fear" in German. We looked at the drawings. They were beautiful. My father liked the idea of me playing jazz with my new wife, and he staked me $20,000 to start a small home recording studio. He had never been so generous. The pianist and I did some advertising gigs and the soundtrack for two of the video adaptations of my dad's books: *Brave Irene* narrated by Lindsay Kraus and *The Zabajaba Jungle* narrated by Fred Guinn.

We also did a recording for a short animation on *Sesame Street* called "Five Baby Oysters," which taught about the number five. We hired Serena, the five-year-old daughter of the great drummer Jimmy Cobb, to do the voiceover. We did a few gigs, but once we were married, the pianist didn't want to play with me any longer. One day, she walked out, and that was it.

In the early stage of that marriage, I stopped getting high. I simply couldn't afford to. The most difficult thing was to deal with the headaches I'd been experiencing since my first accident. Pot didn't get rid of them, but it helped me ignore them. Sifu's Chinese herbs helped my transition to getting straight.

Nine

SOLITUDE

Although my career was going nowhere, my creative output was going way up. I didn't have any producers, record companies, or creative directors telling me what I could or couldn't do. I was out of the loop, but I was free. I started writing music for a flute band. Playing all the parts myself was possible through overdubbing. The biggest problem of being a jazz musician now was finding other musicians to play with. With less work and nowhere to sit in, my flute band became vital in keeping my creative juices flowing.

My bass flute replaced Eddie Gomez. I altered the bottle drum sounds by using my old equipment from the electric flute days. Bill Evans had gotten me interested in writing twelve-tone tunes, and I wrote dozens for my flute band. Twelve-tone music completely changed my sense of harmony. I was alone, but I became a much more complete musician.

I was able to record all the music I was playing every night. I knew that the music was good, so the fact that nobody wanted to give me a gig or play with me had nothing to do with my musical worth.

I don't cook. My diet relied on a nearby supermarket for prepared tray dinners, Chinese food deliveries, and cheap restaurants. I drank a ton of coffee and always had two eggs for breakfast, which I usually ate at around four in the afternoon. The only healthy purchase I made was to buy a juicer for making fresh vegetable and fruit juice.

I had a woman, who would occasionally show up and dump her stuff in my apartment. I met her at one of my gigs. I was weak, and she had pushed her way into my life. She thought she was an artist and made sculptures out of the garbage that she picked up off the streets. She claimed to have hypoglycemic attacks, and when they happened, she would run into a restaurant and stuff herself with food. She gained ten pounds every year.

Depression is last noticed by the depressed, and I had become that. I thought that I was okay because my music and art were improving. I didn't notice that I was living in a pile of crap. A messy house is the most obvious sign of depression. I had been making additions to my equipment, which included what seemed like miles of wire crisscrossing the living room. Nothing had been thrown out since I moved there around 1970. Every drawing of mine, either good or bad, was stuffed into my backroom with Eddie's bass and Don Alias's conga drum.

I think one of the reasons why I didn't notice my own depression was that almost everyone I knew was living in a hoarding mess just like me. When I say everyone, I mean my neighbors and the few friends I had left.

A musician must experience the blues to play the blues. I've had my heart broken and banged myself up enough times. Now I was playing blues in my house. I learned a new lesson in my life: how to play for no one. Art for art's sake. No dreams of fame and fortune. No appreciation from the crowd or lines of groupies—just me playing for myself. I started bringing my flute down to the laundry room in the basement. The acoustics down there were perfect for the flute. This music had only one reward: the music itself.

I always enjoyed my birthday, even though I was often alone. I would spend it listening to the annual twenty-four-hour broadcast of John Coltrane's music on the radio. We share the same birthday. I can't think of better company.

I'd been reading J. Krishnamurti's books for about ten years since my father recommended him. I went to hear him speak at the Felt Forum next to Madison Square Garden in the early '80s. My father told me that he was looking for sainthood when he turned to Krishnamurti. However, he mailed me all the books he had when he couldn't find it. I read them one by one, and Krishnamurti became my newest jazz teacher.

Although he was not a musician, he understood what real creation was, and reading him made me understand my own creative processes in a much clearer way. When you take a bunch of riffs and put them together, that's invention. Creation comes from a blank page. The creator has to get rid of the "me," which is all the facts of his own life or everything that makes up the me. A musician needs to play music without awareness of the self. When the music is really happening, I'm not thinking. Playing music is more about being open to the energy around me.

Krishnamurti covered just about all my concerns in life, but sometimes he talked about drugs. I always skipped that part because I guessed that he wasn't for it. Since I went straight, I've gone back into some of his books and read those chapters that I had previously avoided. He made some good points. He talked about knowing people who had experiences with powerful mind-altering drugs like mescaline. He suggested that drugs could indeed open up doors of perception, but that after the experience was over, those doors would be double-locked. The only way to get back in would be to take more dope. I can attest to that.

The last time I read him, I found out that Krishnamurti hated Picasso. Nobody's perfect.

During the Persian Gulf War in the beginning of the '90s, I left the television on all day and all night, even while I was asleep, to watch its development. I muted it when I was composing or recording. With all the high-tech weaponry of the US military, we were all in for a show. The first night of cruise missiles was a spectacular light show. After that, generals with pointers were calling the operation Desert Storm.

I think that the US government was afraid to show the public too much, like it did during the Vietnam War. The number of strikes, planes, and missiles involved, however, gave my mind's eye a clear and terrible picture of what was happening—mass murder. It was a turkey shoot. I wrote a tune called "Desert Swarm" because I imagined the fighter jets as hundreds of deadly mosquitoes.

Saddam Hussein was evil, so we killed everyone but him. Should all the Americans die for the evils of George Bush? He gave Saddam the money—$1 billion—and the weapons to make him the murderer he was. And supplying that much deadly weaponry certainly qualifies for conspiracy to mass murder.

Around 1990, I got a call out of the blue from Liz, the ex-girlfriend of Racey Gilbert, the drummer from the group I played with in Bermuda. She came to my apartment with her mother who used to be an art dealer. Liz told me that her mother used to sell Picasso paintings in New York.

The mother was excited over my drawings, and she and Liz got this idea of bringing me over to Israel for an art show and concerts. Liz lived there with her husband and four kids. She played jazz piano, but she wasn't very comfortable with standards or blues. Her free stuff was interesting. I gave her some drawings so she could show them to a gallery owner they knew in Israel and forgot all about it.

About six months later, Liz called me from Israel. She promised me two weeks of gigs in Israel and said that I was going to have a show in a beautiful gallery in Tel Aviv. I wondered if I might actually have some roots there. Grandpa had kicked a rabbi in the ass, and Liza was a goy, but I was still 50 percent Jewish, and Dad was a famous Jewish cartoonist.

I packed about fifty drawings and flew to Israel. When I arrived there, Liz told me that most of the gigs had fallen through—shades of Paul Winter in Brazil. She put me in an old hotel and left me there for a good part of my two weeks' stay. The room had a shower and a hot plate for coffee but no television or radio. The place did have a great variety of bugs. Large cracks ran across the walls. The place was ancient, out of a black-and-white movie.

I might have enjoyed it if I had a girl with me, but with the gigs coming at the end of my stay, I didn't have the chance for that. Outside was a road to nowhere. All the buildings were the color of the sand. You might say that Israel is a colorless place. The only thing that kept me sane was the Krishnamurti book I had brought with me.

I tried to check out the political scene by talking to some locals, but all I learned about was the hatred the Jews have for each other. The nonreligious Jews hate the religious Jews, and vice versa. It seemed to me that anyone getting his or her brains baked in that hot sun would eventually go mad.

Liz and I played a gig at the Red Sea Jazz Festival. We flew to Eilat. When I got off the plane, I was hit by what felt like a blast from a giant hairdryer. It was windy and 110 degrees with no humidity. You could see forever. Once I became used to the weather, I found it invigorating, at least at night. The concert went well. A newspaper review said that Liz and I were "the best Israeli band."

At the end of a very lonely and boring trip, I had my show, if you could call it that. The gallery was a nice-looking place with a grand piano for Liz to play. We did a concert for a full house of people, but they were never told that my drawings were on exhibition. The drawings, forty of them, were stuck together on one wall behind the stage. They didn't even have a small sign next to them with my name on it. It was a joke.

A friend of Liz's read dirty poetry with us. The poems were about very horny stuff, like wanting to be ravished by a lot of men. Her husband sat there in the crowd. After the concert, the drawings came down.

On the plane home, my seat was next to a rabbi who smelled awful. When a guy wears a heavy coat in the hot sun, what do you expect? If I could invent a deodorant for rabbis, I'd make a fortune. Before I could pinch my nose and settle in, another rabbi ordered me to change seats with him. He was very pushy. His seat was next to a three-hundred-pound nonreligious woman, and he refused to sit next to her. She turned out to be very nice and didn't smell. I guess I'm not one of the chosen people.

My drawings were in frames, so I had to rely on Liz to get them back to me. It took about six years.

America is the land of drum machines and samples with a loud angry voice on top of them. No notes are needed, and if there is a chord, it's contained in the sample. The irony is I owe my survival partly to a sample. For those who don't know, a sample is a tiny snip of music taken from someone's record. This is then usually repeated for the length of the new piece of music. Hundreds of lawyers specialize in samples.

The Beastie Boys sampled my flute from an old tune I recorded in 1969. You can still hear the scratches off the record it was taken from. This became a big hit called "Sure Shot." It used two bars of my flute. Some people get fifteen minutes of fame—I have two bars of fame. The Beastie Boys did a good job with it. I don't know if I would have survived then without the royalties from the Beastie Boys. I received more money from them than I'd received for all of my twenty albums.

I'm not against the act of rapping. Rex Harrison rapped his way through *My Fair Lady*. Talking blues predates rap. Mickey and Sylvia had a great rap in the middle of one of their songs. What bothers me is that the record companies are using rap to get rid of just about every other kind of music, except for country western. Rap can be added to music just like a sprinkle of salt, but by itself, it doesn't qualify as a complete musical form. Here's a rap record I would like to hear—one that talks about real problems facing all of us, using jazz solos and real drums.

This period of my life might have brought me down if I hadn't gotten my new friend, Frac. Bob Fass, the DJ at WBAI, who is also a cat rescuer, had a six-month old cat named Boom Box, who hadn't been fixed yet. Boom Box made it with a tuxedo cat appropriately named Fred, for Fred Astaire, who gave birth to Fractal (or Frac), my cat. Bob gave him to me in 1995.

Frac brought back love and caring to my life. When I drew, he would sit in front of me surrounded by bottles of colored ink. He examined all my drawings. He slept next to me and woke me up by walking on me and giving me little bites that usually didn't leave any mark. He had a whole language of bites. When he wanted to wake me up, he'd stare at me close up until he caught me opening an eye, and then he'd vocalize.

Frac developed an amazing vocabulary. The most recognizable sounds included "I want water, food, or a clean cat box" and "I want to bite you." He was easy to take care of. He pooped on one side of the cat box and pissed on the other. My only problem with him was that he loved to eat paper—mostly my bills—and he had a jones for photographs. Something about the smell of the photographic chemicals turned him on. I had to keep my photos in the filing cabinet—the only place he couldn't get into. I still have many photos with his teeth marks on them.

I was living surrounded by dead things from the past—old LPs, tapes, reviews, photos, and dusty paintings by various members of my family. Frac represented life.

In 1997, Eddie Gomez, the drummer Eliot Zigmund, and I were invited to play in a big band tribute to Bill Evans in Germany. Bill Dobbins arranged and conducted a bunch of Bill's tunes. I was also hired to do the poster for the concert. I drew for about six weeks straight trying to make the best poster I could. I found it hard to draw a poster of Bill when he was already dead. I didn't play with him so that I could get memorial gigs.

Memorials for fallen jazz musicians have always made me uncomfortable. It happens every day. I just passed by the Blue Note, and they are having a Friends of Dizzy Gillespie show. Last month, the Blue Note had a memorial for Herbie Mann. Bird still gets them. It's a way of burying jazz itself. The headliner is dead, and all the musicians are sidemen. Many bands have dead leaders today: the Charles Mingus Band, the Count Basie Orchestra, Duke Ellington, Buddy Rich, Woody Herman, and the list keeps growing. Who plays in these bands? Their names are in the fine print. The big money goes to the leader, and he's dead. If Bill Evans were here today, I'm sure he would have wanted us to play our own music.

After I sent my drawings, the Germans told me that they received them too late. They used someone else. I was somewhat relieved because I wasn't crazy about what I had done.

We arrived in Germany a week early to rehearse with the band. The rehearsals were held in a large recording studio. The engineer and head of the project was a big, round, jovial, red-cheeked German named Wolfgang. He was the same engineer who recorded my album *Lend Me Your Ears*. The arranger Dobbins was a brilliant man. He had come to Germany three years earlier to conduct the Radio Big Band in Cologne. In that time, he learned how to speak German fluently. His arrangements were outstanding.

I must admit I was intimidated by the situation. Playing with a big band was new in that I had to read a lot of music. With Thad and Mel, I just soloed. I hadn't had to read music very much since high school, and some of the charts were difficult to read. With that many people wearing headphones, the only way to get a good mix was to leave one phone off to hear the live sound with that side. I couldn't do that because I don't have two working ears.

On the rehearsal day for the flute parts, I had an accident. One of the lenses to my reading glasses fell out on the way to the studio. They were hanging around my neck. I didn't know until it was time to play. That was one of the worst days in my life. I tried to look with one eye. I ended up getting nonprescription glasses at the drug store. I played in my hotel every day that week so that my chops at least would be in good shape on the day of the concert.

My section of the concert started with a flute solo. The hall was beautiful with excellent acoustics. It seated about 2,500 people and the house was full. As I started my flute solo, the microphone began to descend slowly. It hadn't been tightened enough. At first I tried to bend down lower, but the mic wouldn't stop, and it went all the way down to my waist. Things kind of went downhill from there. My drug store glasses didn't do a very good job. The only tune I remember enjoying was "Nardis," which we did as a quartet. My big band days were over. I went home with my biggest payday for one of my worst performances.

Ten

JAPAN

Later that year, Eddie Gomez called and asked me if I wanted to do a tour in Japan. We had played in Japan for a week in the mid '80s as a duo, but this time, I was his sideman. He had a trio with Jimmy Cobb and Stefan Karlsson. I grabbed my flute and the only pair of shoes I had and hit the road again.

The format of the music we were playing was rigid. Eddie wanted to make sure that the audience knew that the group was his, so he limited the space I had to play in. I was still happy to be playing with a band. And I fell in love with Japan. Everywhere I went it was clean and peaceful. People were friendly in a respectful way. I became interested in sumo wrestling, which was usually on television before I went to work.

Coming from the cave in New York, I suddenly saw a light at the end of the tunnel. After almost every gig, people of the various towns and cities held receptions for the band, usually with terrific plates of sushi. This was my first experience with authentic Japanese food. Unfortunately, Eddie didn't like Japanese food, and the band ate at Denny's, Royal Host, McDonald's, and Korean barbecue restaurants.

Everyone in the band except me had their own CDs to sell after the concerts, and they made money. I expected that Eddie and I would be able to bring our new duo CD on our next trip. We actually had about five CDs worth of material from the years of recording we had done in my apartment. Eddie refused, saying that the world was not ready for the duo. Having worked on the duo since 1956 and performed as a duo all over Europe in the 1970s, I thought he was being extremely jive. He then suggested that I sell my drawings since I had no CD.

In 1998, I went back to Japan with a new pair of shoes. Eddie told me that he had it written into his contract that his hotels had to always be near a major shopping mall or department store. The tour covered most of Japan, and we traveled every day.

One of the first gigs was in a small city called Morioka in Iwate Prefecture in the northern part of Japan. Before the concert, I accompanied Eddie to a department store and watched him buy clothes and shoes. When we reached the fifth floor, I saw something I wanted— a fountain pen. It was perfect for drawing on the road. The female clerk didn't understand English, and she picked up the phone and called somebody. A few minutes later, a younger clerk showed up to help me buy the pen. I asked if I could try one out on a piece of paper. She handed me the pen, and I did a drawing of a bass player and gave it to her. She spoke English fluently and was very cute. I thought that this was the kind of woman I'd like to live with but someone I would never get to know in my kind of life. Eddie was hogging the conversation, so I suggested to him that he invite her to our concert, which he did. The concert hall was a perfect place to play in with an excellent sound system, but she didn't come.

Back in New York, I hung out with Frac until it was time for the next tour in Japan.

A few days into the next tour, we played at a club that was so packed with people that they had to transfer the band to another club for the intermission. It was only two blocks away, and I didn't wear my coat. I didn't realize how cold it was outside because of all the heat we generated while playing. A few days later, I came down with the flu. My nose dripped for the entire month in Japan. The rest of the band made me wear a mask and sit in the back of the bus by myself.

About a week after I became sick, we were back in Morioka at the same concert hall. I sniffled a lot but played pretty well. We had a reception afterward with great sushi served in a small banquet hall of our hotel, which was near the department store where I had bought the fountain pen the year before. I was going to grab something to eat quickly before retiring to my room when a girl came up to me with my drawing in her hand. She said, "Do you remember me from last year?"

I certainly did. She told me her name, Asako. We sat down together. Not knowing that I was deaf in my left ear, she sat on my left. This proved to be an advantage because I could turn my head into her to hear what she was saying. Fortunately, I didn't give her my flu and kept my sniffling down to a minimum. She said to me, "You must have a very interesting life, traveling all over the world playing music."

I told her that unfortunately, I was out of work most of the time and that she had caught me on a good day. She said that she had kept my doodle from the fountain pen shop on her corkboard because she found it interesting that I had drawn an illustration of a bass player, not a flute player. She mentioned my tie looking Japanese, and I said I had bought it in Kyoto. I said I saw some beautiful Japanese scrolls there. She told me how she was working at an art gallery in the department store (in Japan, each department store has an art gallery) and that she knew some art dealers who specialize in scrolls. She then saw my drawings in a clear file on one of the tables at the reception. She knew an art dealer who liked jazz and said that she would introduce my work to him if I was interested in selling in Japan. She asked if I wanted her email address. I didn't have a computer at home, but I said yes. She gave it to me on a piece of paper. My nose began to run again, and I said that I had to go back to my room. She said that it felt as if she had known me for a long time, and we hugged. On that tour, I actually sold many of my drawings at the concerts and went home with an extra $4,000.

While I was on the tour, Paige, my childhood flute teacher, died. He was living in Texas. He died of leukemia.

When I returned to New York, I used the money to buy my first computer. Up to that point, the only letters I had written in my life were from summer camp when I sent one-line notes to my parents asking either to send money or get me out of there. So writing on a computer to somebody in Japan was a task. I sent Asako an email that consisted only of a drawing and my name. I didn't know that you had to compress a large image file to attach it to the email. She told me later that she had to wait for about twenty minutes to download my email. I sent much smaller images to her next, and she wrote to me. After a while, I had a Japanese art dealer.

When the band came back to Japan in 2000, Asako was working in Tokyo, which made it easier for us to meet. She brought the art dealer and a couple of her friends to our gig in Tokyo. I had a Japanese girlfriend! I kept selling my drawings at the concerts because Eddie still didn't think that the world was ready for the duo. He didn't care because he had a new CD of his own every year. Then came the year 2001.

That year, both tours of Japan were memorials. In the summer, Eddie did a Bill Evans memorial tour, and I saw Asako again. Back in New York in September, I was watching television as usual when suddenly, all the channels switched to the images of a fire in the World Trade Center. Apparently, two planes had crashed into both towers. I watched for a few minutes and turned around to have a sip of coffee. When I turned my head back, only one tower was left standing. New York was encased in thick smoke. I ran across the street to a deli and bought some large bottles of water, closed the windows, and had Chinese food delivered for at least a week.

The day after this tragedy, my doorbell rang. A delivery man with a mask on was standing at my door. I had ordered a book by David Icke entitled *And the Truth Shall Set You Free* that had actually predicted something like this happening. The terrible images of the event filled all the television channels for about ten days. And the more I saw, the more questions I had about the official explanation, which didn't match the visuals. The event reminded me of the Kennedy assassination. Many television commentators compared this event to the Japanese attack on Pearl Harbor, but I didn't. It looked more like an inside job. When a passport from one of the supposed hijackers was found in the rubble, I felt that something fishy was going on.

The only emails I received were from my friends in Japan. They all asked if I was okay. Asako phoned me. That she was able to reach me was a miracle. For the next three months, my telephone was completely dead.

Half an inch of gray dust lay inside my windows at Washington Place. I realized later that parts of people were probably in the dust and wrote a tune called "People Dust."

There are a number of books and videos about 9/11 being an inside job. The incident has been on my mind for years. For a few years following the incident, I avoided riding the subway as much as possible because I thought breathing the underground air was dangerous. I didn't know what matter from the rubble I was being exposed to. We had a friend who had been waiting on tables at a patio of a restaurant in the West Village that day. She complained to Asako and me about coughing spells she was experiencing.

Both Asako and I watched on television (she in Japan, I in New York) people waving out of the windows of one of the Twin Towers when it was about to collapse. We discovered after we married that the collapse had reminded both of us of videos of controlled building demolitions using explosives we'd seen on television. The official explanation about the collapses was that the towers had disinte-grated due to the heat that had been high enough to melt reinforced steel, which didn't make sense to us. How could those people still be alive and waving if the buildings were so hot?

In the winter of 2009, I had a chance to talk to a Japanese archi-tect about it in Japan. A friend of ours knew the architect, and we were invited to spend the night at his home he had designed. He had a beautiful house with a fireplace and a loft where his wife made handwoven fabrics.

The next morning, the architect, his wife, his daughter who had been living in Canada, our friend, his wife, Asako, and I had breakfast together. I asked him what he thought about the collapses. Everybody at the table readily recalled watching similar footage on television and understood why I couldn't accept the official explanation. The architect had to think hard while his daughter kept pressing him to offer some expertise, but he had no answer.

We talked about an American college professor who had his own explanation about the collapses, which contradicted the official report, and how he had lost his job later. Most people I knew in New York refused to talk about 9/11. Whenever I brought up the question about the collapses, they told me that I was out of my mind.

I went back to Japan again in the winter for a Sleepy Matsumoto memorial tour with Eddie's group. Sleepy was one of Japan's pioneering jazz sax and flute players. I never met him. Sleepy's widow sang "*Bésame Mucho*" with Eddie. Two tours in one year turned out to be a little too much for our Japanese audience. We did not have a tour in 2002.

I spent the year by myself with Frac. I discovered that he had great hearing. While I was playing solo on the flute in the kitchen, he came in and sat on my feet. He waited for me to stop and then sang my last note back to me in tune. This went on for about six months. One day, Frac got creative and started adding notes after I stopped playing. Still perfectly in tune, he added up to four or five more notes—always perfect musical finishes to what I had just played and in tune.

On my sixty-third birthday, I played him a new blues I had just written, and he answered back with a flatted fifth. He also hummed in his sleep.

I called Asako in Japan on the weekends. I was enjoying this period of my life. I got to know myself without having to listen to someone else's opinion. I spent a lot of my time throwing out the junk from sixty years of heavy living and forty-two years of relationships. I had a large television, but the media is 95 percent Big Brother and the same crap was coming out of it, so I started reading all the guys who have been kept out of the media: Noam Chomsky, Howard Zinn, Greg Palast, William Cooper, Gore Vidal, and Jim Marrs. I concluded that the plight of jazz was directly connected to the plot of the greedy to take over the world. I'm hoping what I have to say might help a tiny bit in the fight for freedom of thought. That's the next battlefield—your brain.

Asako flew to New York to stay with me for nine days in the summer. I was still cleaning my apartment when her plane touched down at JFK. I couldn't meet her at the airport, so she took a taxi. Near

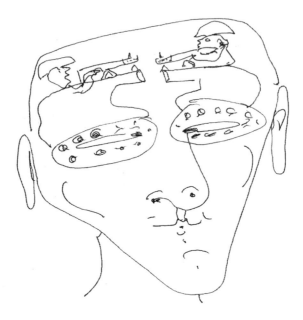

Thirty-Seventh Street and Eighth Avenue, the cab driver drove into a
FedEx truck. Asako smashed her cheek into the divider between the
driver and passenger seats. The ambulance almost drove away with
her, but she asked which hospital they were taking her to. When they
said they wouldn't know until they received a response, she decided
to go see a doctor on her own. She dragged her suitcase by herself to
my apartment.

I took her to the emergency room at Saint Vincent's Hospital, which
went bankrupt several years later. It took about five hours for her to
be admitted. We were stuck in a hallway with an elderly bike rider
with a profusely bleeding nose and several patients on stretchers. One
of the patients said that he had to pee, and the doctor told him to go
ahead and pee right there. That's when I noticed that all the doctors
had rubber boots on their feet, and pee was on the floor.

When her turn came to do an X-ray, it was almost midnight. A
younger doctor said the results showed that she might have broken

her neck a long time ago, which only went to show that they didn't know what they were doing. She was put on a stretcher with an over-sized neck brace and wheeled out into a big room with many other stretchers. I went out to get some sandwiches.

Around two or three in the morning, she was left for an hour or so in a dark hallway upstairs for an MRI, for which they charged $1,500. (She had travel insurance.) Seeing her in that helpless posi-tion felt somewhat romantic because I had always been the one on the stretcher. She wanted to get out of there as quickly as possible.

After about fifteen hours, I took her home with a slightly sprained neck. That was the beginning of my hot date. We had a beautiful week together. At one point, she said that she didn't feel any chemistry between me and Eddie when she saw us play together. I was shocked to hear that, but she was right. The chemistry was long gone, and I was living with memories. We hadn't been partners for years.

The night before she flew back to Japan, I asked her to marry me. Having lived in Idaho as a student, she had no illusions about the wonderfulness of the United States. Her host mother called black people the N-word in 1985. On Sundays, she witnessed white parish-ioners fainting or having seizures in the aisles of the church. In Greenwich Village, someone was always peeing outside my apart-ment building, so I wasn't surprised when she asked me if we could live together in Japan. She had a good paying job in Tokyo. At that point in my life, however, I still had hopes for my jazz career in New York, so I convinced her to stay with me there.

We decided to take a photo of us together holding the newspaper with the date showing. We thought that it would help with the legal process in the future when we actually got married. We set the timer on the camera for ten seconds. While waiting for the flash, Frac ran over and jumped in our laps. When he blessed us like that I knew everything was going to be all right.

I thought I had done a good job cleaning my apartment, but she informed me that it still needed a lot of work. As soon as she left, I began carting numerous garbage bags full of crap out of my place. We stayed in touch by telephone, which was much easier for me than email. She told me that her parents' only concern when she told them that she was going to marry a musician was if I had any debts. I was going to be her first husband, so I had to be introduced to her family.

Asako is not religious at all, but her sister was married to a Buddhist monk, who, at that time, was managing a temple in Maui. Asako and her parents were going to visit Maui during New Year's week, and I was invited along. When I arrived in Maui, the three of them picked me up at the airport. Because nobody was allowed to park in front of the terminal building since 9/11, her father rushed out of the car and called to me, "Jeremy-san!" and grabbed my suitcase. Her mother was in the backseat, cracking up. Asako was driving.

We had a family dinner of mahi-mahi, where I met my sister-in-law and her husband. We visited the temple, and I played some Japanese tunes with her accompanying me on the piano in the main hall. On New Year's Eve, we gave a small concert at the gathering of the Japanese American parishioners.

That night, my brother-in-law performed a New Year's ceremony with firecrackers going off in the background. The temple had a huge bell that could be rung with a log that was about six feet long. The bell was tolled 108 times, representing the 108 worldly desires. I joined the bell ringers and rang it five times.

On January 26, 2003, I picked up Asako at JFK airport—I wasn't going to make the same mistake. Eddie had a Japan tour coming up in the spring, but he didn't have a new CD to sell. He decided that the world was finally ready for the duo. We mixed in my living room studio and

I drew the cover. I put an illustration of me as the flute player on the left side and Eddie on the right for no particular reason—it was just a drawing. But Eddie became upset when my name appeared above the illustration of the flute player and insisted that his name appear first. That was the last straw. I realized that I was about to go on my last tour with him. He must have felt the same way because he came to my apartment to collect his bass after twenty years.

My wife and I married on April 1. The floor we were on in the municipal building was empty except for one other couple, probably because nobody chooses April Fools' Day for a wedding. My wife woke up early to put on a kimono. She had a book of instructions on how to wear kimono by herself. Usually in Japan, brides have another person helping them when they get married. Frac lay in our bed and watched her in fascination. At the last minute, I remembered to buy my ring off a stand in the street. Asako turned her ruby ring around so it looked like a wedding band.

We almost didn't get married on that day because I left my photo ID at home. You must have at least one form of photo ID to enter the building. The young black security guy saw my wife all decked out in the kimono and made an exception.

The ceremony was brief. A middle-aged female official was picking her teeth. She said, "Do you?"

We both said, "I do," and that was it. That was the first time I felt positive after I said, "I do."

Two days later, I took my wife to Boston. My father was on his way out from the world, and I'm glad that he was able to meet her. He looked at our clothes and kept repeating, "Interesting color combination."

We went back to New York the next day, and I was off to Japan. The duo CD was popular in Japan. In fact, I had Asako ship two additional boxes. But my long association with Eddie was over. We had made it through four of my marriages but not the fifth.

While I was gone, Frac made friends with Asako. As soon as I came home, I got sick and stayed in bed for two months. My blood pressure had gone up to 180 over 120. I had a new doctor in Chinatown, after Sifu had passed, who treated me with herbs.

As soon as I recovered, Asako started to clean up the apartment, and I began looking for my first band since the last century. While looking for musicians to play with, I discovered that many of them were teaching in jazz schools. Few could make a living by only playing jazz.

Asako said that I needed a website because nobody knew if I was dead or alive. She built a website for me, and within a week or so I started to receive emails from my fans in different countries. Until then, I had been feeling that I was a total failure. However, the website with basic information about me and my past albums received positive responses, which was unbelievable to me. Many flute players contacted me, asking me about flute playing or requesting a lesson.

In the summer of 2003, I put a quartet together and started to play regularly at the Cornelia Street Café, which was two blocks from my apartment. The band featured Vic Juris on guitar. Concurrently, my art dealer in Japan booked me a gig at the 2004 Yokohama Jazz Promenade along with an art exhibition. He added some extra gigs in the Tokyo area. I had to draw enough pictures for the show, and I became busy. Asako said that I needed a cleaner house to keep my drawings for the show and a decent space to work in. I had my drawing table in the hallway outside the kitchen, so we moved it to the living room, and we threw out more garbage bags of junk from the backroom.

Eleven

THE EGG

On October 3, my father died. He was one month away from ninety-six. He had a favorite story about him and my mother. I don't know if I was even born yet. Liza dropped an egg on the kitchen floor and didn't clean it up right away. After a while, my dad asked her if she was going to pick it up, and she replied, "That egg ain't going nowhere."

I reminded him of that story on the phone shortly before he died. He laughed and said, "The egg stayed there all day."

He had a unique sense of humor.

When I was five or six, he told me that he knew someone who had a yak's penis for a cane. This was around the time he used to read me *Moby Dick* and tales of Robin Hood and Pinocchio. (Liza used to read me *White Fang* and *The Call of the Wild*.) He explained that when a large animal is about to die, it sometimes gets a hard-on. The dick petrifies and can be used as a cane. He told me that some butchers used bulls' penises for canes. I mentioned the yak's penis story to Dad a few years before he died. He said that he had looked all over his house but could not find it. It turned out that he himself was the proud owner of the yak's penis.

He had two small strokes at the age of seventy-five that affected his memory. When he'd tell me that he couldn't remember anything, I would ask him about the guy who was bitten on the dick by a poisonous snake, and he would remember it all. Those jokes were the last to leave him.

In the last months of his life, he could hardly talk, so he started communicating with his facial expressions. His face became an animated cartoon. He was performing with his face. The last thing he said to me was, "Do you know my son?"

Dad turned me on to Reich and Krishnamurti. I turned him on to Monk, Coltrane, Bartók, and psychedelic drugs—a pretty fair exchange.

Twelve

CLEANING UP

n 2004, Vic Juris and I began to record a duo album in my living room to bring to Yokohama. Asako and I moved my bed from the living room and made space for Vic to play facing the recording equipment. I squeezed myself into a small space in the new bedroom. The recording section of the living room consisted of a twenty-four-track board, an eight-track tape recorder for playing half-inch tapes, three racks full of processing equipment, large speakers and monitoring speakers on the stand, a drum machine, Auto-Locator, and two boxes of empty bottles. Most of the equipment was broken or breaking. The thick dust from 9/11 didn't help.

All my windows except the kitchen window were blocked for sound-proofing with half-inch thick Plexiglas boards that weighed a ton. Needless to say, my apartment had little ventilation, and my window to the fire escape was inaccessible. I gave Asako a half-hour lesson on engineering, and we began to record a completely improvised duo CD, with the exception of "Billy's Bounce," a blues by Charlie Parker, and Monk's "Friday the 13th." Frac stayed in the living room.

We had to stop many times because of the various noises—notoriously loud sirens of the New York fire department and police, garbage trucks, idling Mister Softee trucks, and boom boxes—coming from the street. Thanks to Vic's patience, we were able to make an interesting CD, but this was the last time that my equipment would function.

Vic played a steel-string guitar on the CD, but he didn't have an anvil case to check in with his luggage on the plane. After 9/11, musicians weren't allowed to carry large instruments in the cabin with them. Three days before Asako and I left for Japan, Vic came to rehearse with a nylon string guitar and said that he was going to bring it instead of the steel-string one because he had a case for it. But it sounded kind of anemic. Vic wouldn't spend the money on a new case, so Asako went uptown to Manny's Music and bought a flight case for him.

The next morning, we went to the New School where Vic was teaching to show him the case. He checked the case in front of the security desk in the entrance hall and said that the case we got wasn't good enough and that he needed an ATA flight-certified case. Asako and I were flying out the next day, so we went back to Manny's in the rain and bought the last case in stock. We immediately went back to the school to give it to Vic. This time, we went inside the building and saw where he taught. The teaching booth was tiny, just big enough for an upright piano, an amplifier, and two people. The neck of Vic's guitar was almost poking into his student. Vic approved the case.

On September 30, 2004, Asako and I took off for Japan. Well, not exactly. The plane had some problems. Auxiliary power was down, so we had no lights or air-conditioning. And we were made to stay in our seats for four hours.

Finally, the plane was on the runway picking up speed. When we were about to leave the ground, the engines started to cough, and the plane skidded to a stop. Apparently, a bird was sucked into the left engine, and our flight was canceled. We had to stay in an unmade room at a flea trap hotel at the airport—Ramada Inn. The next day, they gave us a plane that flew, and we made it to Japan in time for my performance on NHK radio.

A Japanese bass player and I visited a nursery in Yokohama where my art dealer's son was attending and played for the little kids. The next day, we picked up Vic at the airport. When the art show opened, local television news came to film Vic and me play. A jazz radio program host showed up for an interview. I talked to customers at the gallery in the daytime. Then, in the evening, my art dealer drove Vic and me to our gigs. I had no time to rest, but I enjoyed playing my own gigs. I hadn't done it for a long, long time.

Typhoons rarely hit Japan that late in the year, but one happened during a gig in Tokyo. All the trains stopped. The club was in the basement, and the rainwater seeped through the walls. The majority of the audience who reserved their seats had no transportation to get to the club, but three young daredevil skiers/riders showed up. A mere typhoon couldn't stop those guys. They had used my music for their snow-riding film. Vic and I had an inspiring gig that night.

On October 10, we played the Yokohama Jazz Promenade. The show was recorded and aired on local television later. It took place in one of the early Western-style buildings near the Port of Yokohama. The acoustics were excellent. According to Asako, the promenade didn't usually allow encores because of their tight schedule, but we played one. After the concert, a long line of people who had bought our duo CD was waiting for autographs. Vic kept saying, "Jeremy Steig has left the building," a reference to Elvis Presley.

Asako and I took advantage of this opportunity to have our belated wedding reception with her family and friends. We reserved a room at a pretty good restaurant in Chinatown. Vic said that they served the best Chinese food he's ever had. Chinese food in New York is dangerous to eat.

Asako's relatives came from Hiroshima and had been bombed on August 6, 1945. They were in the city that day except for Asako's parents who had evacuated to the countryside. Some of them still have debris embedded in their bodies.

During lunch, I talked to her uncle who taught English in Japan. He had the experience of being thrown in jail after somebody snitched that he was reading English literature in the toilet during World War II. I told him that everyone on my mother's side had PhDs, and my uncles on my father's side all quit college.

This was the first of my frequent trips to Yokohama. The city is the second biggest in Japan, with a population of almost four million and has the cleanest and safest subway system I've ever seen. Underground supermarkets directly connect to the subway, where I found much better food than the gourmet supermarkets in New York. I could use the public bathroom with my flute under my arm and not worry about being mugged, which was amazing to me. The center of the city has little noise pollution. And we walked everywhere. I never needed a cab with such terrific public transportation; however, if we ever feel like traveling in luxury, a Japanese taxi is a great option. The door opens and closes automatically. The seats are clean, and many drivers wear white gloves. Even though the streets have no signs or numbers, the drivers know them all. And just in case, they all have GPS installed.

Japan has a declining population problem. However, the presence of children is everywhere. I see little kids playing in the street or going to school unsupervised, just like I did in my own childhood. The general atmosphere reminded me of Greenwich Village in the '40s. They also looked a lot happier than the kids in New York.

I also found it impressive that Japanese people have respect for other people's things. I lost my new leather gloves twice in my neighborhood. Both times, someone had picked them up and placed them where I could find them. I would never expect something like this to happen in New York. I had played gigs in different parts of the world, but this was the first time that I wasn't anxious to go home.

Back in New York, my gigs at the Cornelia Street Café continued. The café was not a big moneymaker by any stretch of the imagination. However, with many clubs going under, the café was considered one of the hot spots in the city. I had been off the New York scene for over two decades, and this was supposed to be my comeback. I hadn't been paying attention all those years, which was probably a good thing. I had been depressed enough without knowing what was happening to jazz.

Vic was not the only jazz professor in town. Most of the musicians were making their living by teaching at expensive jazz schools. Their students would go to the clubs and offer a quintet for $100. This automatically set a price for the professional musician. It seemed that every time a jazz spot closed a new jazz education program was born. Parents can burn over $100,000 on their kids' jazz education. When the kids get out of school, they find out that the only jazz for them was back in school.

How can schools teach students how to become womanizing dope addicts, who could transform their feelings into music instead of analyzing them? So students study every Bird lick they can get their hands on in an effort to be the next Charlie Parker. They never will, though, because those licks came from a real person, one who students can never be. Musicians have to look into their own souls and turn them into music, and that just doesn't happen in a classroom.

One night in the early '70s, Bill Evans and I were trading fours, which is to exchange four-bar solos. During that exchange, I played back to Bill something he had just played. Afterward, he took me aside and said, "Don't ever play anything I play."

I should have known better. That was my only verbal music lesson from Bill.

At Music and Art High School—now called Fiorello H. LaGuardia High School of Music & Art and Performing Art—jazz is being taught. What a difference from the days when I used to jam with Eddie and get caught by teachers! I can't imagine these students having their solos graded. It amounts to a teacher judging a student's deepest personal feelings. I'm sure that obedient students get better grades and a chance to advance to the next level, while the kid who got caught smoking weed in the bathroom gets expelled. And that's the kid who might have had a shot at becoming the real article. A real jazz musician must be a rebel. Don't get me wrong—a lot can be gained by studying music, but classical music theory contains all the knowledge necessary to become a first-rate jazz musician. That is, if you have the jazz gene.

Most of the people who played in my twenty-first-century band were teachers. They taught in little cubicles and came to my gigs completely exhausted both mentally and physically. How can one play his best at nine o'clock at night when he has been listening to students attempting to play since the morning?

I noticed another difference from the old days. The band didn't talk to me between the sets at the club. Maybe I'm not very likable, but I had a feeling that they don't communicate with each other either. But plenty of people in the audience wanted to talk to me; they came from all over the world.

You know now why I wouldn't teach in a jazz school, but I was never asked. However, in the several years I played at the café, I found out something interesting. One night, a Japanese lady came up to me after the first set and said that she had won the Jeremy Steig Award at the Berklee College of Music as the best jazz flute student. The same thing happened with another lady at the Blue Note in New York where I was working. Berklee never told me about the award. Which Jeremy Steig are they talking about?

My gigs also attracted people from my past—young and vibrant once but now older and bitter. Time is not nice to many people, especially people from the '60s, it seemed. Most of them couldn't take the culture change, and it showed. My old girlfriends showed up and didn't know how to be just friends. They showed up to listen to me play but had no interest in reconnecting with me as a person. Asako videotaped each one of my gigs at the café and I kept introducing her to them, but nobody knew how to talk to a younger person from a different country. I realized that I had become a different person too.

The videos of my own gigs inspired me to make a CD of the quartet. We recorded some standards along with my own compositions at a professional studio in New Jersey. The CD is called *Flute on the Edge*.

Until Asako obtained a work permit in the United States, we both kept cleaning whenever we had a chance. One day, she said, "What are you going to do with this conga drum?"

Don Alias had left it in my pad about fifteen years before. We decided to find Don. In November 2004, he came to pick it up. I had a terrific time seeing him again. As soon as Don met Asako he asked her if she had a sister. Same old Don. He had been playing with David Sanborn and invited us to their gig at Blue Note that night. Don played beautifully.

We went out to a sushi place nearby between the sets. He told me that Sanborn had a new producer who tried to show Don what he wanted him to play by beating on a table. Don said, "What do you think you're doing? You can't tell me how to play the drums. You're not a drummer."

As a result, he was left off the CD, he said. His eyes were fluttering as he spoke, sipping his beer. Don had recently collapsed on stage and he said that he had gone into a coma for two days and almost died from hypertension. Sanborn was going to Japan, and he couldn't go with him. I asked him to come to the café and play with my band in December.

Playing with Don again was great. I kept bugging him to go to our Chinese doctor so that he could get some herbs for his high blood pressure. I finally took him just before Christmas and bought him an electric herb pot for a present.

He couldn't make the next gig at the café in the middle of January because he was sick. I wasn't able to reach him for a long time, and when I did, he was on a plane. He was on the way back from his son's wedding and sounded very happy. Not long after that, Don died.

At the wake, my album *Energy* was playing. Don was usually hired for his excellent conga playing, but with me, he played the drums. *Energy* was one of Don's favorite records. I remember walking by

Washington Square Park with him. He had a small set of Moroccan drums under his arm, and I had an Indian flute tucked in my belt. Don started playing something funky with his free hand, so I whipped out the wooden flute, and we played while we walked. He could make special things happen.

About the same time, Ghost, the self-taught flute player in the East Village, died of cancer in Los Angeles, and five months later, we lost Frac. This drained all my energy.

In the fall of 2006, I had an art show with a duo concert at the Unison Arts Center in New Paltz. Cameron Brown played the bass with me. At the concert, I saw two old Satyrs: Warren Bernhardt and Adrian Guillery. Adrian had gained about 200 pounds. He knew it was me but hardly spoke. His roommate told me that he would sit in the house and eat pizza all day. Adrian once wrote a tune called "Pizza Man." The words I remember were "I'd rather eat pizza than be your lover man."

I had found one of Adrian's electric guitars from the '70s while excavating my backroom. He had painted and decorated, transforming it into a psychedelic masterpiece. Next time I worked upstate with Vic, I brought the guitar and returned it to Adrian. Vic saw it and said that he wanted it.

I realized that I had some unfinished business. The eight-track tapes of my flute band had been sitting in my hallway for fifteen years. I decided that it was time to make a CD of them, but I ran into trouble right away. All the tapes were sticking together in the reels. I contacted the only person I knew of who could still repair a professional tape recorder.

When he came he told me that the only way to fix my tapes so they could be mixed was to have them baked in a special oven. This would cost me a fortune, so I thought that I would buy new tapes and do it all over again. That's when I got my next shock: nobody was making tape anymore. This meant that practically all of my equipment was now worthless and unusable. Almost everything I owned had become obsolete. Asako and I spent about six months unraveling and chopping tape off the reels, separating the metal from the tape.

One evening, we left the twenty-four-track console outside our building by the garbage. We took a walk in the Village and came back about half an hour later to find a young kid taking a picture of the board with his cell phone. We went upstairs and looked out of our window. A car pulled over, and two kids loaded it in the back and drove away.

The next night, I took the eight-track tape recorder out to the street. It rained that night. I couldn't believe that I had once paid $5,000 for it. I think that kind of thinking is what creates hoarders. Hoarders think they can't throw anything out that might be worth something.

I was starting to get a thrill out of tossing my stuff. My hoarding disease was cured. Asako was brought up in a very small apartment in Japan, and every year end her family would throw out unnecessary items so that their living space was maintained. She was a wonderful help to me.

I had always been exceedingly proud of my family and displayed them everywhere in my pad. We took their paintings off the wall, cut them out of the frames, rolled them up, and put the frames out on the street. Their art had been staring at me all my life, and once they were gone, I realized that so many things had angered me about my family. I had been trying to see only goodness in them, but in reality, they were an extremely oppressive bunch who didn't want their children to equal their accomplishments. Getting my family off the walls was liberating.

My friends and neighbors used to frown on me for having such a cheap rent and not taking care of my place. Now they hated me for having a big spacious apartment at a cheap rent.

I tried going into a studio to record my flute band. I hired an engineer I had worked with in the past, but it turned out that he had not been able to make the transition from analog to digital. After wasting a few thousand dollars, I canceled on the engineer and regrouped. I took a chance that it didn't really take ten minutes to create a new track on the computer as it did with the engineer and bought a set of digital recording devices, all of which fit on a single table.

Even with the consolidation of space with the new equipment, the backroom of my apartment didn't have enough space for recording, so I gave the orgone box away. I'd had it for forty years, and giving it away marked the completion of the cleanup. I felt that I was ready for a new life.

I bought seven thick books on how to operate my new equipment. I didn't think I would ever get through the manuals until I realized that I only needed to learn one-fifth of the content in those books to do what I wanted to do. For example, the books explained how to store every note played, including the mistakes. This kind of information was important only if one couldn't play one's instrument well. In my case, all that needed to be done was to click on Destructive Record, which would eliminate the wasteful saving of garbage.

Digital recording equipment is great, but most of the CDs these days aren't about music. Rap and technopop depend more on computer tricks than musical knowledge and skills. The most important trick is the loop. That's how my flute was used on the Beastie Boys CD. By taking a small snip of music, people can loop it or make it repeat as many times as they want.

While Asako, who had begun working as a full-time translator, worked in a small workspace in our bedroom, I recorded in the backroom. We would meet for lunch in the living room, which was now open enough to play Ping-Pong in. I had found out that it took only about ten seconds to create a new track. Not having to depend on a band or engineer was wonderful. I did have to depend on Asako for the stereo mix because I have only one working ear. The CD is called *Pterodactyl*.

Toward 2008, I gradually lost interest in playing at the Cornelia Street Café with my quartet. After almost four years, I was tired of playing with the band that never talked to or hung out with me. I could see from the videos that we weren't developing musically: my band remained Jeremy and the Tired Professors. New York had ceased to be the vibrant creative place I grew up in. When Blue Note rereleased a recording I did in 1969 with Don and Eddie, the All About Jazz website sent me an email indicating that they would review the CD if I had an upcoming live performance. I wrote back saying that the three of us would never play together again and that whether they reviewed me or not was their business. Incidentally, on the sleeve of that CD, Blue Note credited my father for my line drawings.

I began to think about getting out of America. Asako and I had been going back and forth between New York and Japan, and coming back to New York was no longer exciting. After spending a couple of months in Japan, the stench in the streets of New York was incredible. I felt ready for a change. In my eyes, America had had its day. When my father-in-law became sick, we decided to live permanently in Japan.

No one I knew could readily believe what I was about to do. After all, America was the most wonderful place in the world. That's what people seemed to think, no matter how miserable they were, especially in New York. In my own apartment building, tenants were being thrown out because they couldn't pay the rent. When we said we were moving, we were inundated with requests to sublet our apartment. When an old acquaintance of mine who had been living in Florida left a message on our answering machine asking us to sublet, I could hardly believe it because we hadn't been in touch for years. We couldn't sublet legally, so we said, "No." People were upset about it.

I'm very outspoken politically. When I compared America's wars in Iraq and Afghanistan and the torturing of uncharged detainees to the Nazis, everyone turned a deaf ear to me or tried to shut me up. I realized that speaking English didn't help me communicate with other Americans, which made going to Japan, without knowing how to speak Japanese, much easier. I was ready for a brand-new life. We took our last plane out of New York on June 27, 2010.

Thirteen

MARCH 26, 2016

thought that this book was an accurate account of the jazz life going up and then down.* My concerns have all become reality, and I haven't even touched streaming music, the final nail in the coffin for the music I love so much. The good thing is jazz will always be with us. It's in the air. No computer can kill that. One day, some musicians will discover that it was standing right there next to them and the process of collective improvised music will start all over again. I won't be there. I have cancer, but as Howlin' Wolf used to say, "I have had my fun."

---

* Jeremy put down in handwriting the thoughts in the next few chapters while he was back in his hospital room at night. (He did things at home during the day.) He asked Asako to add them as the final chapters to his story. He also asked her to add her view of their life together to conclude the story.

I tried to sell this story. Everyone loved the information and the list of famous characters, but the main criticism was that I didn't pour my heart out when I had the chance—like when I found out that my father was fooling around with my second wife. I just said, "That's nice."

I could have said that it broke my heart, but I thought that anyone reading would put himself in the same position and feel my pain. In music composition, that's called the understatement. Anyway, too late. In this final chapter, I have plenty of pain to talk about.

I have now moved to Japan. My wife's father got Lewy body dementia and we moved so we could be with him and my mother-in-law, Akiko. He got sicker very fast, and we had to put him in the hospital. He was pretty much a vegetable lying in a room with three other patients. The feeding tube kept him alive for three years in terrible pain. He had a very strong heart. Still, moving to Japan turned out to be the best thing we could do. First of all, I think it saved Akiko's life. Trying to take care of her husband, she was in a terrible depression, and we stopped it. She rented an apartment in the same building my wife and I were living in. We ate our dinners together, and we went on trips to beautiful places in Japan. I've had four mother-in-laws previously, and they fit the crappy mold, but Akiko is different. She's very special. I will tell you more about her later.

Just before my wife's father was too impaired to sign his name, he sold me a studio apartment he owned, which was a seventeen-minute walk from our place. That became my music studio.

We live in Yokohama. There is no music scene here, and I soon realized that some big life changes were needed if I was going to survive creatively in Japan. I had ideas about stories for children but never did anything about them. After all, my dad was the creator of *Shrek!* But I had done soundtracks for some of my father's stories. Asako and I wrote four sketches of kids' stories. They weren't anything like my dad's stuff, and I had an idea for a three-dimensional stage with the characters cut out. We made something we called Styrofoam Theater, which was made of Styrofoam and glue. It cost us $7. Before leaving New York, we had been noticing that children weren't walking anymore. They were being pushed around in carts, and they looked very sad. That became the theme of our first story, "Don't Strap Me Down."

The day that we finished making "Don't Strap Me Down," our condo in Japan began to shake back and forth violently. Japan is prone to earthquakes, and we had a plan to get under the table, which we did. It shook for five minutes. Every twenty seconds or so, I said, "Oh, shit."

The whole sentence would have been either "Oh, shit, we're going to die" or "Oh, shit there goes our investment on the condo." We had purchased a huge television. It crashed to the floor. We picked it up, and it still worked (Japanese technology). All afternoon, we watched the tsunami on television.

At first, the tsunami was incredible to watch. Then we realized that thousands of people were dying. Next, we saw the nuclear plant blow up on television. A few hours later, we started getting email messages from New York urging us to come home. We wrote back that we were staying put. New York was going to get something like Hurricane Sandy. So what's the difference? One lady who didn't even like us wrote that we could even stay at her house—a fate worse than death. When we didn't accept her offer, she wrote back basically to tell us to go fuck ourselves. After that, we never heard from anyone in New York again. And that is the number one reason I love living in Japan. I've been able to leave my life in New York forever. I finally know peace.

Fourteen

MARCH 27, 2016

Okay, literary agent, I'm in the hospital. Tomorrow, I get heavy chemotherapy. I just had a biopsy. It felt like I was being raped with a dry broom handle and a staple gun. I guess that was to get samples. They already know my cancer has spread to my liver, but they have to determine what kind.

"That's nice."

My lips have been numb for about ten days, and I don't know if I'll ever play another note on the flute. "Nice." Well, back to my Japanese experience.

Asako and I got really good at our stories. We call them digital picture books. She designs sets, does the photography, and edits everything, including the stereo mix of the music. Being deaf in one ear, I can't do that. She also does most of the voices and the translation between Japanese and English. I do the illustrations and the music. She is the best partner I ever had. We even discuss the stories while walking or sitting in the bathtub.

In Japan, I've been devoting my creative time to doing things I believe in. We've been making videos of our trips, which I then compose music for. It's been a wonderful experience for me. I even started playing free piano. The musicians here have a lot of respect for me but don't want to play. That's better than New York, where there is no respect and no playing. Anyway, the piano helps.

Four years after coming here, I took Asako to the Blue Note in Tokyo to see the Average White Band for her birthday. She bought a couple of their LPs when she was a college student. Our table had a Jim Hall plaque embedded in it. The whole place was in complete darkness when the band hit the first note. It startled our waiter, who was standing right next to our booth with a bottle of water and two glasses on the tray. Before we knew it, our table and seats were soaked with Perrier. The music and food were very bad, so we decided to split. On our way out, they double charged us on our credit card though we made it clear that we had already paid when we made the reservation online. (When we got home that night, there were a couple of messages from Blue Note Tokyo on our answering machine, apologizing for the double charge and promising to return the money.)

The night was still young, so I took Asako to Body & Soul, the place I always finished my tours at with Eddie's quartet. The club owner was happy to see me and offered me a gig. I told her that I hadn't met any musicians in four years but I could still play. She made a phone call, and ten minutes later, I had a band. The club was packed and stayed packed for the seven gigs I played there until the end of last year. It turned out I really had some fans. I learned how to design better sets. I got to play all of my Kotato flutes, including the bass flute in F. I even played "Friday the 13th" and "St. Thomas" on my piccolo. Before each gig, Asako and I ate dinner at a Japanese Italian restaurant, which was better than the expensive Italian places we used to go to in New York. I guess I'm retired, but I went out with a bang. The last tune I played was "Straight No Chaser."

Fifteen

MARCH 28, 2016

oday I learned that I have about two weeks to live. I hope I have enough time to find the good recordings I did at the Village Vanguard with Bill Evans. I cry a lot, mostly that I won't have the wonderful company of my loving wife. I'll also miss playing my flutes, drawing, the great food Asako and Akiko cook every night, walking in Yokohama, and the cherry blossoms.

I won't see Trump or Hillary become president. I won't get to see America become a police state or Japan fight a war. I won't get to see the next tsunami, earthquakes, erupting volcanoes, mud slides, and floods, not to mention the next nuclear accident. I won't get to see what Asako will have to witness.

Part II

ASAKO'S STORY

Sixteen

NEW YORK

After I saw Jeremy for the second time in 1999, I kept having this inexplicable strong feeling that I had known him for a long time. Neither of us could think of any reason why I should feel that way, but I did. Looking back, it was a case of *unmei no akai-ito*, which in Japanese means that your pinkie is tied to your soul mate's pinkie with a red string. The string, of course, is invisible.

I had met few people in Jeremy's life before I moved to New York. But not knowing anyone there wasn't a problem for me. I wasn't bothered by the idea of being thrown into an environment where I knew nobody. I had been a foreign student staying abroad temporarily on several different occasions. I had learned to maintain a delicate balance between being a part of everything and keeping a distance.

When I was young, Japan simply wasn't interesting enough for me. Everything was implied, and I didn't want to pretend to get it all the time. I had a vague dream of leading a rootless life: have a job that pays the bills and hopefully move around and live in a few different countries without worrying about marriage or planning for a family. Unfortunately, however, my dream wasn't meant to be. I spent almost all of my twenties fighting a pretty severe skin allergy. I actually had to move to the countryside for a better natural environment. I lived there for about six years. For the last three years, I jogged about three miles every morning before going to work and finally recovered my health. When I got my face back, one of my coworkers said to me, "I never knew how you really looked."

I met Jeremy when I was a jogger.

As I got older, I developed a fairer view of the world, and I wasn't exactly thrilled to move to New York to settle down there, but it wasn't a completely unacceptable idea either.

When a couple of old friends of his in New York learned of his plan to marry a younger Japanese woman (Jeremy was senior to me by twenty-six years), they let him know how they felt about it. One woman told him that she had been sexually abused by her father, who, after having kids with her mother, ran off with a Japanese woman from Okinawa and left the United States, abandoning the entire family. Jeremy said that she had never told him about it for the decades he had known her. Another woman reminded Jeremy that she had two kids with her husband, who divorced her and married a much younger Southeast Asian woman in California. Jeremy also told me that a Caucasian male piano player with whom he had played often in Japan asked him how he could marry someone with a completely different ethnic and cultural background. I was surprised to hear such a concern because I was under the impression that jazz musicians in general were more cosmopolitan and told Jeremy so. He said, "I guess not," and smiled wryly. I thought that these old acquaintances of his forgot to be diplomatic perhaps because of the trauma they had suffered or their strong disapproval of my nationality and ethnicity. This presented a striking contrast to all my friends in Japan, who congratulated us on our marriage. Seven of them as well as my parents came over to stay with us or visited us while we were living in New York.

The two of us concluded that our marriage must be grossly unpopular among those who had known Jeremy for a long time. He jokingly said, "It's because I was the most eligible bachelor in the neighborhood."

I got a kick out of that.

I was used to people being themselves around me. So why make waves? I just made sure not to be impolite to them. Besides, my focus was on the two of us. Just about the only friend of his who made a refreshingly positive comment was Jean Ray of the folk duo, Jim and Jean. She said on the phone from Colorado that I was lucky because Jeremy truly was a one-in-a-million kind of guy.

On June 13, 2004, she came to visit. I took a picture of her and Jeremy sitting side by side on the piano bench. We went to a sushi place nearby, but Jean hardly ate. She was extremely skinny. I don't remember what she and Jeremy were talking about, but at one point, she said out of the blue, "I hate fat people," and repeated it.

Jeremy and I sensed that she was very sick and was in New York to say good-bye to her old friends. I felt bad, as if I were throwing a monkey-wrench into the works by being there. She probably preferred to reminisce alone with Jeremy. We parted on Sixth Avenue. She said she was to meet more friends uptown. She seemed to try not to show too much emotion. Jeremy said she was very pretty when she was young. That day, she had her long hair down like a young girl. I could almost see her in her twenties. About a year later, when Jeremy sent her an email to see how she was doing, she was already gone.

I remember one particular case in which my being Japanese helped. When I moved to New York, Jeremy had often been getting harassing phone calls in the middle of the night. The female caller was supposedly a magazine reporter who got Jeremy's phone number to do a story when he was on tour in Germany, but she turned out to be an overzealous fan. She would sing songs into his answering machine at two in the morning. I erased his answering message and recorded a new one in Japanese. When she called the next time, we let her listen to it. When she started to call out to Jeremy through the speaker, I picked up the phone and told her that I was a Japanese person who'd just moved to New York and that I had recently been given a new phone number. She told me that Jeremy, who used to live at that number, was her close friend. I said, "I'm sure this close friend of yours will give you his new number soon," and hung up. She never called Jeremy again.

I was getting introduced to everybody as his wife, and Jeremy liked that I used his real name to refer to him. I heard his sisters, ex-wives, and old friends use Jemmy, his nickname from childhood, but he just wasn't Jemmy to me. He and I were building a new life together, and I felt that it had nothing to do with who he might have been to them. I think he had been feeling that he had to do something about his life but needed a boost. My arrival in New York did the job, which probably seemed totally out of context to everyone around us. It made sense to only the two of us. Life is like that.

Jeremy had a phone conversation with his father in Boston almost every day. William Steig stayed alive for only six months after Jeremy and I got married, but I vividly remember Jeremy repeating himself on the phone because his father would ask him the same question every two minutes during the conversation. "How are the Knicks doing?" was the kind of question he would ask. They were both NBA

fans. Jeremy liked basketball because, he said, it had the most improvising of all the sports. I was impressed with Jeremy's patience with
his father. I didn't think I would call my parents up every day if I
expected to put up with repeated questions. Jeremy didn't seem to
mind at all. He seemed to be genuinely happy to talk with his father.

One time, I said to Jeremy that I didn't understand why his father
had left such a nice, talented son. My father was always home—in
fact, I can't remember him not coming home for dinner—he was
always around. I had memories of us going fishing, playing ball, and
solving math problems together. Jeremy had none of that. Once or
twice, he told me about a winter coat his father had bought him
on one of his weekly visits when he was a teenager. I said I found
it ironic that the world believed William Steig had a great understanding of children. He was a famous children's book author, but,
in fact, he was a lousy father. I also said that it was wrong that the
world knew Jeremy as William Steig's son because he didn't raise
him. I said that everybody should give Liza more credit. Besides,
she was the one who saw that Jeremy had musical talent. In my
mind, Jeremy Steig the flutist wouldn't have existed if it had not
been for Liza. I remember Jeremy saying, "I'm afraid he (William)
wasn't a very good father." Then he said something insightful: "My
father was able to write those books because he never grew up. He
was a child himself."

Jeremy threw up violently a couple of days after he had received
the news of his father's death. Back then, I didn't have the slightest
idea how I would react to my own father's death, so I just stood by
him without being able to offer any kind of wisdom about how to
cope. Jeremy didn't draw for about six months. He said that he used
to draw because drawing made him feel connected to his father. I
think it was a hard time for him because he had just begun to plan
his 2004 art show in Japan.

Ten years later, when my father died, I didn't have any regrets because he and I used to talk daily. At the funeral, I just said, "Catch you later," to Dad, who was lying in the coffin. I didn't even cry. When I look back, I see that the experience must have been completely different for Jeremy. I always wonder if his life would have been better if his father had been around.

Almost every morning, Jeremy would watch the news about the war in Iraq in the living room. While I was getting our breakfast ready in the kitchen, he would walk in to reveal his thoughts on international affairs and US politics. In Japan, I knew nobody who talked about politics on a daily basis. Most Japanese people prefer to avoid it altogether. I was relieved that Jeremy was vocal about politics. I also loved that he was against the war. He especially couldn't understand the so-called liberals who tried to justify violence. He was concerned about what's happening in the world, which to me was proof that he was a sane individual. At the same time, I didn't want to have such a bad impression of the United States—after all, I had just migrated all the way from Japan—so I asked him to hold off on talking about Colin Powell and Condoleezza Rice, at least till after breakfast.

At first, Jeremy showed little interest in eating. Every morning, he made a tall glass of fresh organic vegetable juice with a heavy-duty juicer. "For my health," he said. Other than that, he drank many cups of coffee. His mug was huge by my standard. Open bags of Pepperidge Farm strawberry jam cookies sat in the living room. I moved to New York in the winter, so I cooked hot food for every dinner. He wasn't picky about food. He had toured in Japan many times, so he didn't have any problem with Japanese dishes like miso soup. He just didn't react to my cooking very much, and about two weeks later, I didn't know what else to cook. I had fallen into a "dinner depression." He didn't even eat at regular hours, which made me wonder if he cared at all if I made dinner every night. I was stuck, so I asked him what he wished to eat. To my surprise, I got an immediate answer: "A salad."

It turned out that he loved fresh vegetables with enough dressing to pour over them on the side. He especially liked avocado slices with balsamic vinegar.

If an average Japanese person were asked what dish would typically define a dinner at home for newlyweds on a cold winter night, the answer would probably be *oden* (vegetables, fish dumplings, tofu, and other ingredients stewed in a stock) or *nabe-ryori* (a hot pot cooked at the table). That, however, wasn't the case with Jeremy. Inside our apartment, the temperature was kept quite warm, thanks to the central heating system. Jeremy had a T-shirt on while outside was freezing. He also was barefooted in the house most of the time.

As soon as he requested a salad, I thought of a green salad with French dressing and a potato salad with small apple pieces in it. I also quickly went over a niçoise salad recipe in my head. But those three salads would take care of my dinner depression for only three days.

I rushed to the bookstore a block from our place and bought a salad recipe book. I read in the introduction that the most important thing about making a salad is to toss it in an oversized bowl right before eating. I made a trip to a kitchenware store on West Broadway and purchased a huge plastic salad bowl, made in Italy. (I still use it and love it.) From then on, I made a different kind of salad every night, and soon Jeremy was making comments.

The book had a variety of salad recipes that called for chicken, roast beef, tuna, eggs, and beans to make it the main course. I had never built an entire dinner around a salad. This style of meal was completely new to me, and I started to have great fun cooking for both of us. Jeremy was happy to try new salads, and I was cured of my dinner depression. Soon after, he offered to wash the dishes after every meal. He kept that promise throughout our marriage.

We took long walks in Manhattan. We'd had very few opportunities to go on dates due to the physical distance between us. One time, we ran across the guitarist Jim Hall on Sixth Avenue. Jeremy introduced me to him. After that, I often saw him at the fish section of Jefferson Market while grocery shopping and told Jeremy about it afterward. He really liked that I had neighborly encounters with the jazz legend. Jim was very friendly, and I thought that he was a gentleman. He was one of the first people who phoned to offer condolences when William Steig passed away.

When Jeremy wasn't doing anything, he would draw. He didn't have any problem talking and listening while making pictures, no matter how serious a subject we might be taking up. We all do things while breathing. For Jeremy, drawing wasn't that much different from breathing. After all, he had spent hours doing it every day since childhood. And he seemed to have so much fun with it. Some people, however, didn't know how to react. Not too many adults draw all the time, especially when people are around. They probably felt ignored or left behind when he kept drawing in their presence. Kids, however, were completely different. They would stand next to him and gaze interestedly upon what was being drawn. They didn't seem to feel walled off by him. Over the years, on at least six different occasions, I saw Jeremy invite a Japanese child to draw by giving him or her a pen. One time, it happened in a restaurant where a friend of ours had brought her daughter to have lunch with a group of adults. The kid happily joined Jeremy in drawing and had a great time until the adults were ready to go home.

His drawings were a manifestation of his unbroken creativity. When he played the flute at home, he did so for hours without a break as well. He said that playing the flute was about telling a story.

He just kept at it. He usually recorded what he played during the day and listened back at night. He was extremely self-sufficient in art and music. All he needed were his flutes, recording equipment, and drawing materials. He was able to have fun while entertaining me for hours every day. I had a great time! All I had to do was to cook what we liked to eat and pick up around the house so that we could work in a clean, organized space without aggravation. He always said to me, "I didn't marry you so that you would cook and clean for me." I knew that, and I explained to him that I would do everything all the same even by myself because I liked to live in a clean house and couldn't stand eating out or getting take-out food every day.

The one place in the house that I never cleaned was his drawing table. Jeremy had his own configuration, and I never touched his drawing materials.

Spring came, and we got married on April 1, 2003, at the Manhattan Municipal Building. It had a gilded statue of *Civic Fame* at the top, which usually looked like a fluttering flame of gold from the ground level. When I was in college, I waited on tables at countless wedding receptions where a huge amount of food was routinely wasted. Most of the Japanese brides I saw looked rather ridiculous in their rented wedding gowns. I wanted a simpler wedding for myself. Jeremy and I didn't even talk about buying wedding rings, but on the day, he said that the ceremony would go smoothly if we had them ready and asked me if I had a ring. I took a ruby ring that my mother had given me to the ceremony.

Two weeks later, he left for a tour in Japan. I stayed home with Frac for three weeks. Instead of being swept off my feet with however I might have felt on a honeymoon, I was given the time to think to myself about what it meant to be married. This was very good for me. Quitting my job and leaving my country had been a big move, and I needed to keep cool. The funny thing was that the biggest headache to me was that our apartment was facing north. To welcome me, Jeremy had replaced his thick old curtains with new white lace ones, but it still felt quite dark inside our apartment even around noon. (My apartment in Japan was facing southeast and had ample sunlight.) We lived in a historic building that had been built more than a century before. Except in the kitchen, the ceiling wasn't wired for lighting. All of our rooms had floor lamps that created an atmosphere in the evening, but the rooms were poorly lit all day long. The lack of natural light was depressing to me. But as there was absolutely nothing I could do about it, my solution was to accept the dimness.

Being alone in the house, I took a good look at Liza's oil paintings and William's drawings on the walls. I could see that Liza could really paint. Her canvases were hanging bare, and they needed to be dusted, but they gave the living room a classy look. I loved the vintage look of the parquet floor of our apartment, but I saw worms (not termites) moving in a couple of gaps between wood pieces. I noticed them because one day I saw Frac staring at them. I used a house cleaning detergent to kill them and oiled the floor.

At night, I either read books in bed with Frac or did a jigsaw puzzle on Jeremy's drawing table while listening to music. I had just joined the New York Repertory Orchestra as second fiddle for fun, and we were scheduled to play Tchaikovsky's Symphony No. 5, so I listened to it on CD. Frac would walk about on the jigsaw patches that had already been pieced together. He and I became good friends.

I needed to work. According to our immigration lawyer, the law stipulated that the Immigration and Naturalization Service should grant a work permit to each green-card applicant ninety days after it issued a receipt for his or her application fee. Since the terrorist attacks on September 11, 2001, however, that law hadn't been observed, our lawyer said. An applicant could get a permit as soon as the ninety-day period was over if he or she was willing to be among the first one hundred to wait in line each morning downtown at 26 Federal Plaza.

At around eleven o'clock at night on July 20, 2003, Jeremy and I arrived there. We brought with us the necessary documents, towels, umbrellas, pillows, a picnic sheet, pieces of chewing gum, a couple of books, and portable reading lights. We saw a line forming along the block and were met by a volunteer who was making a list of the first one hundred of the night. We came in fifty-eighth—we had made it. He said that if we wanted to use a restroom, we had to walk across Broadway to a Kinko's copy service store, so we didn't drink much liquid.

We read and talked through the night. At around five in the morning, the sky paled in the east. We were already tired, but the long day was only beginning. Around 7:30 a.m., we all stood up to form a straight line to where the stop sign was in front of the building. All of a sudden, the man who was standing right behind us went into convulsions and fell hard on the concrete pavement. He looked like he could be from Central America. The impact of the fall must have split his head open. The street quickly turned red with his blood. We just stood there and watched him being picked up by an ambulance.

At 8:30 a.m., we were finally allowed into the building to submit our papers. After that, for roughly seven hours till they handed me a laminated work permit at three o'clock, we were made to sit and wait in a room that was air-conditioned like a refrigerator. We were not allowed to stand up, walk about, or use a cell phone. If you did any of these things without permission, uniformed staff would walk up to you and say, "No." The floor we were on didn't even have a restroom.

Although we were among the first one hundred in the overnight line, we followed the legitimate group of applicants who had officially been summoned to appear that day. So we were made to wait forever. Once people stepped out of the building, they were not allowed back in. We had no choice but to remain in the same spot no matter how cold the room was. Some applicants ran out of patience and approached the counter only to be scolded by the clerk in charge. He said through a microphone, "Those of you who are here on a first-come-first-served basis should know that you'd have to wait." His tone was pretty nasty. Having gone through the whole process, which took nearly eighteen hours, Jeremy and I both wondered if my migrating to the United States was worth all this trouble.

They really didn't make it easy to obtain my green card. For example, on April 14, 2004, I went to Chelsea Village Medical for a checkup, which included something quite unbelievable. I don't know if they still make you do it, but I was required to back then. I was shown to a little room where I was told to undress below the waist and stand with my legs apart. Then a man in a white gown, possibly in his twenties, came in. He bent over, looked up at my crotch, stood upright, and said, "Okay." That was it. They didn't explain what it was for. My guess was that they wanted to make sure I didn't have an unnatural organ down there. On the way home, my thoughts drifted to the movie *The Crying Game*.

I came home and told Jeremy what had happened. He was drawing as usual. He said, "Really?" and let out a sigh of disgust. He then quietly said as he kept running his pen, "I apologize for my terrible country."

Having received my permit, I had two choices: seek employment in Manhattan or work from home as a translator. I first thought from the perspective of a typical Japanese person with a four-year college degree plus an ordinary level of aspiration and found the former to be quite motivating. Then I stopped to really think. *Jeremy, who was sixty, had gone through his fourth divorce a decade before. At one point, he decided he'd never marry again. Yet he brought me from overseas and married me. He must want to spend as much time as possible with me for the rest of his life. That would be the case if I were he*, I thought. So I decided to work at home. Thus we became a pair that would spend twenty-four hours a day together. While I translated during the day, Jeremy would mostly play the flute and record. In other words, his flute playing was the background music to my work for hundreds and thousands of hours.

My job took advantage of the time difference between New York and Tokyo. The translation agency in Tokyo would upload my assignments on the company's intranet at the end of each day. An assignment could be up to either three thousand English words or six thousand Japanese characters in volume. In a couple of hours, it would be time for me in New York to get up and work. I would complete my assignments by five or six at night, which would be the morning of the next day in Tokyo. I offered the fastest way for the agency to render translation services to its clients. My assignments could be in either direction—from English to Japanese or the other way around—and ranged from company newsletters, corporate environmental reports, magazine articles, employee manuals, user instructions for cosmetic products, and PowerPoint presentations to haiku poems. I didn't have a specialized field.

One time, I translated a court deposition by an employee of a Japanese motorcycle manufacturer. A Japanese man had to testify about a model of motorcycle that was involved in a car accident in America. The agency gave me three days to finish. I looked at the assignment and thought I needed to buy a dictionary of mechanical terms. I asked Jeremy to accompany me to a Japanese bookstore near Rockefeller Center, which gave us another chance to explore the city together.

Whenever I had a Japanese-to-English translation assignment that didn't involve confidential materials, I asked Jeremy to go through it. It always helped to get a fresh pair of eyes on what I'd just translated. After a while, he said to me, "How can you get yourself interested in different topics every day?"

I frowned and laughed at the same time and said, "You don't know how lucky you are to have discovered the flute when you were a child. You found something you're great at and love to do very early in your life. I'd love to translate only the stuff I love to read about, but that's just not how it is."

Using a sports term, Jeremy called me a utility player. He commented that the agency must be very happy to have someone like me working for them. He wasn't wrong in thinking that. I once had lunch at a Tokyo restaurant with the head of the agency. She told me that only one out of roughly fifty applicants she interviewed for a translator position stayed with the job. The rest would usually quit within a week. She said that most applicants failed to meet the deadlines because they didn't have a supervisor around. She also said that many of the applicants seemed to overestimate their language skills until they got an assignment.

People usually expect a translator to be knowledgeable, but the most important thing a translator must remember is to be humble. She always has to remind herself to question her own choice of words. And she must at all times check the facts, look up the words in the dictionary, and pay attention to what the author means, which is very difficult. When I told this to Jeremy, he said that being humble was also important for musicians.

One of my regular assignments came from a music label, which was one of the top five in the industry back then. Sometimes they would discuss jazz. For instance, they lamented the forever stagnant sales of their jazz CDs. One of the reports said that even Miles Davis CDs didn't sell any longer. And that was around 2005. Another said that jazz accounted for less than 1 percent of the whole CD market. I was puzzled to learn that this company was going to introduce a system where their musicians would be required to write and submit at least two new tunes per week to the company. When I mentioned that to Jeremy, he couldn't believe it.

One day, he stepped outside while I was working, so I played some old CDs that I had brought from Japan. When both of us were home, we usually listened to classical music (from Bach to Ives and Takemitsu), Jeremy's jazz collection (many by Billie Holiday and Coltrane) and blues like Lead Belly and Robert Johnson, so I rarely played pop and rock CDs from my teenage years. When I put those CDs on, the tunes I thought I had liked didn't appeal to me at all. Rather, the CDs all sounded too weak, simple, and boring, and I laughed at myself for having bought them. I didn't think I would listen to them ever again. I got rid of them when we packed to move to Japan. My Van Halen LPs barely survived this elimination. Living with Jeremy must have affected the way I listened to music. Having heard him build harmonies by overdubbing or play twelve-tone music for many hours, I have probably trained my ears to listen the way they'd never done before.

Jeremy thought of himself as an improviser, not necessarily a jazz musician. One time, I had to work on the *Prelude to the Afternoon of a Faun* for one of the orchestra's regular performances, and I put the CD on to check to see how a certain section was played. Jeremy jumped in with his flute and improvised over the piece, which sounded amazingly beautiful. I honestly thought he made the piece sound better and that even Debussy might have given him a break. I asked him to do it again, and he said that he could never play it the same again. I didn't have a problem with that because I knew that he would play something just as beautiful. Living with Jeremy, I started to think that "genre" was an excuse by and for an incompetent musician.

I kept going to the weekly orchestra practices, until I couldn't because I was too busy with translations. As a child, I learned to play the violin first by the Shinozaki method, but halfway through it, my second teacher forced me to switch to the Suzuki method and start over again from "Twinkle, Twinkle, Little Star." I went through the method and played a couple of additional concertos before I quit playing at seventeen. Later, I took up the instrument again and was a member of an amateur pops orchestra in Yokohama till I moved to live with Jeremy. In New York, I had a new problem. I was a bit embarrassed to practice in the presence of a real musician. To Jeremy's ears, my playing could only be dreadful noises at best.

When I was ten, I told my parents that I was ready to quit taking private lessons if they preferred to spend their money on something else. Young as I was, I already knew that I wasn't going to amount to anything in music. I told that story to Jeremy and asked him to be patient while I practiced. He found it amusing that I had said something like that at ten. A while later, he suggested some things I could try to improve my playing. For example, he pointed out my irritating playing habits while listening to a recording of me practicing. Then he said, "You're not as bad as you think." He could never be completely terrible to anyone. In any case, I couldn't ignore my critical ears. Living with Jeremy, I clearly understood that there are people who were born to play music and that I sure wasn't one of them. This freed me from feeling that I should play or must practice. I guess I had never been able to face that playing music didn't give me that much pleasure. I played my violin less and less, and I really didn't miss it. I don't think Jeremy did either. I don't play at all any longer, and I think the world is a better place, at least by a tiny bit.

Jeremy rarely criticized other musicians' playing. When they asked him for his opinion, he would just say that he wasn't a critic. He would, however, reveal his thoughts to me when he saw my honest reaction to a new CD or a concert we'd just heard. This was very educational. What I found most interesting was what he said about the jazz flute CDs that had been handed to him by the performers themselves at his gigs. He said that they weren't "reaching out." I asked him what he meant. He explained that those flute players recorded what they had practiced many times till the day of recording. In other words, they recorded only what they already knew they could do.

"What's the point?" he said.

Playing music and doing art can be physically demanding. His health was one of my main concerns. When we got together, he was habitually taking strong headache pills. He was suffering an aftereffect of the broken neck from his second traffic accident, which had happened about twenty years before. When his neck or back was out, he had to go see his chiropractor uptown. It happened quite often. He would make an appointment to get his back popped and his neck adjusted. Our insurance policy didn't cover the treatments, and they were quite expensive.

In the spring of 2005, his neck was hurting so badly that he had to keep holding his head with both hands. He went to get treated, came home, and said that the chiropractor had told him to chill the back of his neck with an ice pack, which left me perplexed. This advice was exactly the opposite of what I had expected to hear. In Japan, when people experience pain from old injuries, they usually heat up the affected part—by getting a hot-spring cure, for instance. Anyway, the chiropractor had already gotten Jeremy to make another appointment to explain a new set of treatments he wanted to try on him. On May 18, I accompanied Jeremy, who was still in excruciating pain, to the doctor's office.

We were sitting in the waiting room and saw a Japanese couple come in through the front door. They seemed to be in their late thirties. I could hear them talk in Japanese. The woman said, "I don't understand why the doctor asked us to be here today. I thought we had told him that we were moving."

They were also saying something about catching a plane in the afternoon. They were called in before our turn. A little while later, we walked into a small room with a plastic model of the vertebral column hanging from a metal stand, where we sat next to the Japanese couple on a bench with our backs against the wall.

The doctor came in and talked to the four of us for about twenty minutes. Several times I glanced at the couple out of the corner of my eye, who were itching to leave. I didn't say anything. Jeremy was in so much pain that he was breaking into a cold sweat.

The two of us were then taken to the room where Jeremy usually got his treatments. The doctor showed us a couple of X-ray photos of Jeremy's neck and back and said that the treatments so far had fixed the bilateral S-curve in his spine, but it caused his neck to bend forward by roughly three inches. He wanted to correct that with traction and that the starting price was $3,600 for a twelve-week program. *Is he serious?* I said to myself. That was the most outrageous and ridiculous thing I'd ever heard. I suspected that the doctor had brought in the Japanese couple to prevent me, Jeremy's Japanese wife, from expressing apprehension about his therapy. I thought that the doctor could be using some kind of ethnic corralling tactic to keep Jeremy as his patient.

Back in the waiting room, I told Jeremy about the couple's conversation I had overheard earlier. We decided that we'd never go back again. Luckily, Jeremy had an old friend who had become a Rolfing practitioner. We called him, and he gave us the number of a Japanese-Brazilian shiatsu practitioner. Her studio was within walking distance from our place, and Jeremy started his regular visits. After that, he never experienced severe neck pain. We even took weekly rehab yoga lessons for a while at the same studio. Switching to shiatsu also weaned him away from headache pills. It actually didn't take him long to completely stop taking them. I think that it helped him lead a truly creative life. We also kept up our daily walks in the neighborhood. About three years after we married, neighbors started to mention his healthier look. By the time we moved to Japan, Jeremy had gotten rid of most of the pains that impeded his everyday life.

When my father, in Japan, became very ill in 2009, I said to Jeremy that I wouldn't be able to cook for him every day since I might have to travel back and forth between the two countries. Jeremy said, without much hesitation, "Let's move to Japan."

He said he didn't have to live in New York any longer. He wasn't bothered by the idea of leaving the city.

While we were getting ready to move back to Japan, I reached a turning point in my life. When I was in seventh grade, the teacher of my modern Japanese class asked us, "Why does a person keep a diary?" I didn't have an answer, so I decided to experiment. By the time I moved to New York, I had a large cardboard box full of notebooks that contained about thirty years of my life story. I looked at the box, which would have to be shipped back to Japan. I went through pages and pages of my handwriting. They were the records of what I did, felt, and thought from the time I was twelve. I sought the answer I hadn't been able to find as a junior high school student. *What's the meaning of all this? Is recordkeeping the reason why people keep journals?* Then I realized that the box full of notebooks was evidence that I at least took a moment every day to reflect upon myself. I concluded that I, as a person, was the result of that practice. As for the facts that had been put down, I didn't see much value in them. I mean, I hadn't started a revolution or anything. I set aside the most recent journals that covered my life with Jeremy and shredded the rest. This made me feel extremely liberated. I also felt good about the life-sized me.

Our shredder made a significant contribution to our move. It helped us in clearing out Jeremy's cabinets filled with old documents and faded photos. We bought the shredder downtown. On the way home from the store, we were walking up Broadway when a young woman stuck her head out of the car window and yelled at us, "An excellent choice! I have one too."

She had seen the box Jeremy was carrying and wanted to let us know that she, too, used the same model. That cracked us up, but she was right. This shredder really was powerful.

I was lucky not to have shredded my most recent diaries. In 2016, Jeremy passed away about a month after his condition took a sudden turn for the worse. A couple of days later, I felt as if our time together had been a dream. It wasn't that I had lost my memory but that none of it seemed real. I wasn't even sure if Jeremy had existed at all. So I read my diaries every night. They covered my life from about six months before we got married to the present day. I was short of sleep for weeks but was quickly able to overcome my amnesia-like feeling. This is another important reason why one should keep a diary. Videos and photographs wouldn't do. They are too alive to look at so soon after death.

Seventeen

JAPAN

Our home in Yokohama was very quiet, and Jeremy really took it easy. I sometimes wished I were in his position. Nobody got mad at him for not picking up the phone. Everybody knew that he spoke little Japanese. He loved his studio, which is about a seventeen-minute walk from our home. We didn't install the internet, television, or telephone there so he could concentrate on creating music without any disturbance. Nobody knew he was there. It gave him total relaxation. He always looked forward to playing gigs with a rhythm section, but he had already decided that his flute band was how he was going to create the way he really wanted. He enjoyed working on Pro Tools and did a lot of overdubbing by playing all the parts by himself. He walked to his studio even on a rainy day and played the flutes from morning to night. Sometimes the studio got too sunny for him. I guess he missed the nocturnal atmosphere of our apartment in New York. We went to Motomachi, one of the best-known shopping streets in Yokohama, and bought a cute small electric lamp with a buffalo calf shade. He placed it near a framed copy of a four-panel cartoon by Bill Evans. A couple of times I saw him playing surrounded by the warm color of its light with the curtains closed.

Shortly after we moved to Japan, Jeremy thought of the Styrofoam Theater. We bought Styrofoam boards at a DIY store and assembled a miniature theater. Jeremy then drew the heroine of one of our first stories on a piece of paper and asked me to cut it out. When I did, it made a huge difference. The character suddenly came to life, and we immediately felt attached to it. We pinned it down with a sewing needle in the theater. It looked so cute that we had a hearty laugh together. Jeremy wanted me in charge of cutting. I thought, *I don't have to be an artist to cut along the lines.* Thus, our collaboration began.

Our stories had already been taking shape in New York. Most of them were inspired by the things our neighbors did or said to us. Our neighbors in the apartment building in New York were typical. For example, some neighbors knocked on our door to ask us favors when we began to have ample space in our apartment after we had done some heavy cleaning. One neighbor asked us if she could dump in our hallway the books that she wasn't supposed to have bought. Another was dead serious when she said that she wanted to live in our apartment while we were on a trip to Japan because, we figured, she couldn't stand her husband. A college professor asked us if she could borrow our vacuum cleaner because she didn't have one. My reaction was "She should go buy one herself," but Jeremy gladly let her use ours. What a nice guy! The Southeast Asian lady above us liked to feed the pigeons on her fire escape. She would throw dried squid legs coated with an orange-colored spice, pieces of which landed right outside our window along with some pigeon droppings. These neighbors gave us ideas. Once we learned that we could model our characters after them, observing them became fun.

Initially, Jeremy wasn't sure if he wanted to draw for our stories, because each character's face needed to be repeated identically. Like his flute playing, his approach to drawing was more improvisational. He also said that his late father hadn't been very happy about repeating the same face over and over again for his children's books. Another problem was that we didn't have a realistic idea about how to combine all the elements (his flute music, drawings, and our stories) together. But the idea of the Styrofoam Theater inspired him so much that he was ready to try. He did a sketch of each scene so we could figure out what materials and tools we might need. We went to an art supply store and purchased colored paper, handmade Japanese paper, glues, inks, paints, scissors, and so forth and made everything by hand. We were like elementary school kids in craft class. I photographed the scenes and made an experimental slide show on our PC. It looked like a three-dimensional picture book.

Jeremy was of course in charge of soundtracks. Once he heard what he liked in his head, he would overdub catchy melodies and beautiful harmonies every day with amazing energy. He usually knew in the morning that he would have something ready for me to listen to later that day. I would walk over to the studio in late afternoon and sit down with him to listen. If we felt like adding some vocals, we would experiment. When both of us liked the outcome, we'd start editing. When the day's work was done, we'd discuss the next scene while walking to the grocery store. He was very pleased to be able to write many tunes that set off the scenes. Creating soundtracks in the summer turned out to be quite a job for him because the air conditioner had to be switched off during overdubbing. He wanted to make sure no noise came from it. He would come home for dinner after taking a bath at the studio.

I set out to be just a cutter, but once everything began, I had to contribute more. While Jeremy worked on the music, I set up scenes in our miniature theater and photographed them. Assembling each scene required some attention to details. I had to check to see if the paper cutouts had smooth edges for close-up shots. I also looked for visible unevenness from paintbrushes and glue. The first story came out a little sloppy because I wasn't aware that I had to do all these things. I learned to do better each time we did a new story.

Our stories are short and run for less than ten minutes. We read in the paper, however, that today's average internet users don't stay on the same website for more than three minutes. That's not enough time even for our free-of-charge jazz travelogue videos. People just weren't going to give us the minimum time we needed to express ourselves. It meant that we saw little to no demand for what we were doing. At first, we thought about designing our website for cell phone users to increase our potential viewers, but we figured it wasn't worth the effort. Interestingly, after a while, we found ourselves not caring too much about whether we had an audience or not. We were doing the stories because we wanted to. We grew addicted to the sense of fulfillment we felt each time we completed a story after months of hard work. After each piece, we said to each other, "Never again!" But a couple of months later, we always felt like doing another one. Jeremy thought that the outcomes were much better than he had expected and kept telling everybody about our stories.

We did eight stories in six years. Jeremy continued to work on the storyboard and new characters for our ninth until a couple of weeks before his death. He used to say, "It's not easy to wear so many different hats," but he really enjoyed doing everything. We kept talking about each scene until we were totally on the same page. Jeremy knew exactly what it took to create from scratch. After all, he had improvised on the flute and made records since he was very young. I, however, got my first taste of creating something. I don't mean that I felt like an artist myself. I knew how to operate some electronic equipment and was lucky enough to be able to suggest to Jeremy a vehicle to present his new work. It so happened that our production involved some circumstantial handiwork on my end.

On March 11, 2011, the earth shook. The Great Eastern Japan Earthquake had hit. In our area, it measured 5+ on the Japanese seven-stage seismic scale. Jeremy and I were reviewing our first story on the computer display. Eight months had passed since we moved to Japan. Our condo and his studio were unscathed, but a nuclear meltdown occurred in Fukushima. Jeremy, my mother, and I watched on television Japan's Self-Defense Forces choppers hovering above the nuclear reactors as they aimed to dump some water on them. We felt that staying farther away until things calmed down wouldn't be a bad idea. Jeremy couldn't believe that he happened to be so close by when such world-shaking events as the Three Mile Island accident, the September 11, 2001, attacks, and the 2011 earthquake in Japan happened. He thought he should add his experiences in Japan to his memoir, which he thought had been finished on his move to Japan.

Some may consider it an irony that we went to Hiroshima to stay away from the ongoing radioactive contamination in Fukushima, but in fact, it felt strangely appropriate to the three of us. The United States made the glaring mistake of harming and killing civilians including many children with nuclear bombings. Then the worldwide nuclear proliferation began, prompting the United States to promote "the peaceful" use of nuclear energy, a policy and slogan under which Japan also keeps its nuclear power plants going. And we could see that there was nothing "peaceful" about what was going on in Fukushima. Japan had obviously committed a colossal nuclear blunder. The whole incident presented a perfect opportunity for me, my American husband, and my mother, who had lived in the burned-out ruins of Hiroshima after the war, to visit the city together. As Jeremy mentioned, both my parents are from Hiroshima City, and many of my relatives are hibakusha. On the day the bomb was dropped in 1945, both my parents, who were in fourth grade, had been evacuated. They came back to the city about a month and a half after Japan had surrendered.

The three of us visited the Hiroshima Peace Memorial and saw everything on display. A miniature replica showed the area within a kilometer's radius of ground zero. My mother explained to Jeremy that her house was situated right outside the circle. This shocked him greatly, and he said he wanted to interview her to add her story to his memoir. (He kept bugging me about interviewing my mother, but I never got around to sitting down with him to interpret his questions for her, which I regret. When he learned of his cancer, he expected that one day he would rather stay home than go out. He was saving some projects to work on when that time came, but he passed away before working on them.) This time was my third visit to the memorial. In the renovated building, understanding what had happened was much easier. I was glad that Jeremy got to see the new memorial. He had played in Hiroshima before, but all he had seen was the hotel and club.

My cousin drove us to Onomichi where Jeremy found some bamboo pens at a small stationery shop in a local mall. He had been looking for good bamboo pens since he moved, so he bought them all. We also took a trip to Itsukushima Shrine, a UNESCO World Heritage site. We also enjoyed the Hiroshima Museum of Art, where we were the only visitors on a weekday morning. We stayed in Hiroshima for four nights and returned to Yokohama.

The meltdown in Fukushima remained a hot topic for a while. Around the same time, we often saw a middle-aged woman on Yokohama's subway who had a habit of repeating the same sentences over and over again in a very loud voice, startling passengers in the compartment. For example, she would say, "I have an appointment with my beautician at eleven." Then she would ask, "At what time?" as if two people were talking to each other. She kept repeating the two sentences over and over. Everybody either stared at her or tried not to look in her direction. One day, she was saying that the underground mall connected to Yokohama Station used to have an entrance to a big department store in it and that it was later replaced by an electric appliance store. Jeremy and I often went there for his audio equipment. She described the transition just as I remembered. Jeremy asked me what she was saying. I said, "You know, she isn't as out of it as she seems."

I explained to him that she was actually incredibly accurate about the changes that had taken place in the underground mall. That inspired us to make a new story, "Where Is Julian?" Many people around the world expressed their disbelief and anger at Tokyo Electric Power Company (TEPCO) after the 2011 disaster. The company's explanation that the huge tsunami was unforeseeable and that the company wasn't responsible for the nuclear accident didn't make sense to many, including the two of us. Seemingly sane people could say completely illogical things. We thought that the woman on the subway, in fact, might have a much righter mind than the TEPCO executives. So we did a story about a young boy who seeks after truth. Jeremy drew a psychedelic sunrise scene, which cracked us up because its hallucinatory feeling was perfect for the eccentric story.

Train travel is very convenient in Japan. Jeremy had toured all over the country, but he hadn't done sightseeing. So we took the bullet train to many places from Yokohama. In 2012, we went to Kobe and saw how the city had recovered from the 1995 Great Hanshin-Awaji Earthquake. We made trips to the Mount Fuji area, Nagano, Kyoto, Izu, Okayama, and Shikoku to enjoy nature and hot spring baths. Jeremy decided to record what we saw on the trip, create soundtracks, and make short videos to upload onto his website. I had always been the photographer between the two of us, but that changed in Japan. He knew what he wanted to record and held the Handycam himself much more often. He loved moving water, Japanese koi, birds, and clouds in the sky. He would make a hush gesture with his forefinger and recorded the murmuring of the brook, the raindrops forming little puddles under the eaves of a Buddhist temple, and so forth. He specifically wanted to make a waterfall video, so we went to Nikko, a city famous for its falls and beautiful lake.

As the family tour planner, I looked hard for a room with a view, and we ended up staying in slightly luxurious rooms, such as one with an ocean-view bath on the balcony or another with a private hinoki bath overlooking a lake. I can still see Jeremy sitting in a tub brimming with hot water, with a contented smile on his face. He was very much inspired by nature—it's evident in our travelogue. This was a part of him that I didn't get to see when we were living in New York. We occasionally enjoyed traditional Japanese performing arts like kabuki and kyogen, but his primary interest was in the nature around him. Whenever we took a walk in our neighborhood, he would stop at the sight of striped mullets, turtles, cormorants, and herons in the nearby river. He also loved the cherry blossoms in the spring. He liked Yokohama because he could walk everywhere and experience all these things first-hand. We usually walked for more than an hour whenever we went out.

We grew plants in our shady L-shaped garden that stretched along our apartment. We planted three varieties of roses. In New York,

Jeremy used to grow avocado plants by the window, but in Yokohama, we were able to take the pots outside. Beautiful common bluebottles flew in and laid their tiny pearllike eggs on avocado leaves. We also grew two blueberry bushes and made blueberry muffins in the summer. Jeremy helped me put up a net to guard against birds. He became interested in bonsai at the gardening shop we frequented and purchased a small Chinese quince and a Japanese maple. Using a pair of tweezers, he planted some moss at the foot of each tree. He also shaped each branch of the quince by coiling a wire around it. He especially liked the quince. We called it Jeremy Jr. We took photos of its blossoms every spring, some of which appear in one of our digital picture books. I was a little surprised when he asked me to trim the trees. He wasn't comfortable cutting branches "because the tree is alive," he said. He was like that. He wasn't too happy about being stared at by the eye of a grilled fish on his dinner plate. He didn't like anything that caused physical pain either to himself or another person. He often said that he would definitely have died in Vietnam if he had been drafted because he thought hesitating to take life would have meant his own death in that war.

When we were living in New York, he always kept his flute in sight unless it was locked in a safe or the like. That changed in Japan. About two years after we moved, he no longer took his instrument with him even when we were gone for several days. He wasn't worried about being robbed any longer.

Did he have any stress? He probably did when he sat down with me to learn Japanese. I wanted him to know the minimum Japanese necessary for him to survive a disaster or an emergency, but learning a foreign language at seventy is not easy for anyone. He liked to practice writing Japanese characters, but he would add eyes, arms, and legs to them and turn them into funny cartoons in no time. I sometimes complained to him saying, "Come on! Be serious." He did learn to write simple sentences in the drill books. I respected how he carefully followed the stroke orders because even Japanese people often ignore them. He was able to carry on everyday conversations at the supermarket and with the coffee vendors where he became a familiar face.

We usually ate with my mother, who had been widowed in 2013. Jeremy had invited her to join us to keep her spirits up. My mother contributed at least one homemade dish every evening. She didn't feel comfortable joining us empty-handed. He often took photographs of our dinners before starting to eat and had me upload a bunch of them to his website. Some of his fans saw the photographs and said to him, "You eat well!" when they came to a Tokyo club to hear him play. He was very happy about it.

After every dinner, Jeremy would quickly throw a drying cloth to my mother, saying he was helping her keep her reflexes. They made this their daily routine. My mother admired Jeremy for washing the dishes after each meal. I said, "He has been doing it ever since we got married. He is a much more thorough dishwasher than I am." "He is like God!" my mother exclaimed. She wished all Japanese men were like him.

He connected with my mother, who doesn't speak English, through food. They happened to share the same preferences. They both hated those tiny little seeds in grapefruits. They preferred their tomatoes in their salads peeled. They loved their thin Japanese beef steaks. He loved my mother's potato dishes and black beans cooked with sugar. Living in Japan, he rediscovered the pleasure of eating. He was crazy about Japanese strawberries and peaches and looked for stores where fresh, juicy ones were sold. He became an excellent shopper and even suggested dinner ingredients to me.

My mother was also greatly impressed to see Jeremy drawing pictures or composing on the keyboard before dinner almost every night. She saw that he really loved what he was doing. She is a calligraphy student, and Jeremy, without realizing, inspired her to work harder. Truly creative people affect those around them just by being there. To support her effort, Jeremy and I went to see her calligraphy scroll in one of the annual exhibitions in Tokyo's Ginza.

When my mother was around, Jeremy called me Mako-chan, my nickname from childhood. Only my family and relatives call me that. I don't remember exactly when he started doing it, but it certainly made my mother feel that the three of us were family. He seemed to enjoy the togetherness in his own home. I liked the way he said "Maaah-ko-chan," with an exaggerated "ah" sound.

He was always busy, but he liked to watch television too. He used to watch the NBA games live on television, but in Japan he had to record them because of the time difference. During the season, he would ask me to check the sports section of the newspaper every morning to see if the game results had already been printed, in which case he had to avoid the article to enjoy the recorded games. He came to like British murder mysteries on cable television. We used to watch American dramas in New York, but we both agreed that characters were more real in British shows and the acting was more convincing in general. We liked that they didn't try as hard to be politically correct. I think both of us thought that British people shared a more mature sense of humor.

One murder mystery we watched had an English cop criticize America for having given a reason for the world to sympathize with "Japs" by going ahead with the nuclear bombings in World War II. Jeremy and I were sitting side by side. I turned to him and said, "I've never heard that one."

I then frowned and chuckled at the same time, thinking, *Boy, the British really go all the way, don't they?*

Jeremy gave me a resigned smile and said, "Maybe we shouldn't go to England."

Then we laughed out loud.

Jeremy did watch American action movies with violent explosions and loud gun shots after I went to sleep. He would hurriedly lower the sound as soon as I got up to go to the bathroom.

Eighteen

FINAL YEARS

I n the last gigs of his life, Jeremy enjoyed playing standards with instruments that were rarely featured in jazz. One of them was the bass flute in F, which usually sat on a special stand behind him, waiting to be played. According to Mr. Kotato, the maker of that instrument, Jeremy was, so far, the only jazz flutist to whom he had sold a bass flute in F. He said that Jeremy was the first one whom he heard playing a melody on that instrument.

The first Kotato Jeremy had purchased was a bass flute. Mr. Kotato had also made a special support for the instrument so that Jeremy could play it standing. On February 13, 2015, he played a quartet gig in Tokyo. That night, one of the tunes he played was "Ol' Man River" from the musical *Show Boat*. He played it on the bass flute. The tune was perfect for demonstrating the instrument's full, rich sound. In the middle of the tune, the club owner walked over to me and whispered, "Look, those women are crying."

I cast my eyes along the small tables lined up on the far side of the bandstand and spotted a woman wiping her eyes with a handkerchief. Everyone was sitting still. The whole club was listening.

On our cab ride home, I told Jeremy what I saw. He said, "Yeah? That's nice. It's a good tune to play on that instrument."

Jeremy didn't play to the audience. It seemed to me that music was how he was in touch with himself, and I saw many people reacting to it. I couldn't even begin to fathom his nonverbal, mystic inner world, which was one of the reasons why living with him was stimulating and educational. The funny thing was that he used to say that I knew the art of living. I gave him a doubtful look whenever he said it. I make faces often, and he enjoyed it. All we knew was that we were very different and that we really enjoyed each other's company.

While still on the topic of spiritual aspects of an artist's life, I've noticed an interesting trend in the music world. Classical musicians who are able to play jazz are obviously a big deal. Jeremy was approached for advice by several classical flutists who wanted to play jazz for money. I asked him a couple of times why they wanted to play jazz. One time, he said he really didn't know. Another time, he said, "Well, they all want to prove something."

From a layman's point of view, that trend makes no sense because classical musicians can probably still do so much with classical music. Jeremy and I went to classical music concerts in New York and usually ended up listening to somebody snore among graying audience members.

In Tokyo, we encountered an incident that made me think that Jeremy had touched on a truth when he said classical musicians wanted to prove something. This Japanese classical flutist won an all-Japan classical flute competition. He openly said that, as a young student, he had tried hard to copy Jeremy's solos from the LP *What's New*. We had a chance to hear him in Tokyo at a concert that took place in a small venue. One of the pieces he played was "Flight of the Bumble Bee." When he finished playing the tune, a member of the ensemble who was seated behind him on stage jokingly yelled, "You could play it even faster, couldn't you?" And the flutist made the whole audience sit through the same exact piece we'd just heard. Jeremy and I had never seen anything like that.

A female European classical flutist in her forties often sought advice from Jeremy while we lived in New York. We went out for dinner one time in Chelsea. She was a nice person. She seemed very sincere about music. She finally released her first jazz CD in America after we had moved and kept in touch with us for a while. She seemed to be struggling with her career every time she wrote.

One day Jeremy said that he'd written to her saying that attempting to succeed as a jazz flutist wasn't worth it and that the most important thing in life was to find somebody who really cared about her. It was around 2012. A while later, he told me that she had written back to say that she'd met a great guy. He didn't hear from her again.

In March 2016, we learned that we didn't have enough time left to complete our latest story. He asked me to work with a friend of ours to finish it after his death. We had previously worked with her on "Dizzy and Luigi." She is an illustrator and my high school classmate. She also is the only person who had sent us handmade greeting cards and birthday cards every year. Jeremy always used his original drawings on greeting cards and emails. Things crafted by friends are much more powerful and heartwarming than anything bought at a store. I have treasured the illustrated letters Jeremy gave me before we married.

He was very calm when he learned that he had a week or two to live. When the doctor told me that shocking news in Japanese,

I turned to Jeremy, who was sitting with his back against a pillow, and immediately repeated it in English. I didn't hesitate at all. The doctor didn't expect me to do that while he was still in the room and couldn't hide that he was taken aback and said to me, "I didn't think you'd tell him that now, here."

For me to hold back such an important piece of information, even for a moment, would have been totally unfair to Jeremy, I thought. He must want as much time as possible to do as many things as possible.

We were told that we could go home and do whatever we wanted. Jeremy quickly changed back into his regular clothes. We took a cab home. He was able to walk thanks to the painkiller he was taking. He said that the hospital food would kill him and he wanted to eat fresh vegetables, so I fixed a green leaf salad with some avocado slices on the side. He kept eating three meals a day with me and drawing at home until nine days before his passing. He always said that your time was up when you stopped creating.

He got his last haircut a week before he died. When he came back to his room from the hospital barbershop, he stood in front of the mirror and shaved his beard himself. Then he said, "That made me feel better."

It pains me the most that his continuous creativity has been terminated. He always kept drawing and playing the flute. Of course, I feel the deepest grief every time I remind myself that I will never be able to exchange words with my beloved husband and best friend. It happens when I see his pair of shoes that have stayed in the same spot by the entrance door. It happens when I see the empty couch every time I come home. But it is even more devastating to know that the person who was so driven to create is no more.

Jeremy used to stick a bamboo flute under his belt whenever he went out. He wanted to be ready to play anytime, anywhere.

One afternoon in 2005, he had his favorite colorful Guatemalan vest on and played the flute in the kitchen of our New York apartment. Frac quietly listened at his feet. At the end of each phrase, Jeremy stopped, bent his head down, and stared at Frac's face. Frac responded by meowing back to him. I filmed their exchanges on our Handycam.

After Frac died in 2006, Jeremy would occasionally wonder aloud if he would see Frac again when he died. Remembering that, I placed the Guatemalan vest on Jeremy's chest as he lay in the coffin. Then I put two of his bamboo flutes in one pocket and Frac's whiskers in the other. We had brought them wrapped in a piece of paper from New York. That way, Jeremy would reunite with Frac as he played the flute, I thought. Flowers in shades of orange surrounded his face and body. Orange was one of his favorite colors.

On July 31, about twenty of us left port on a double-deck motorboat. It had been pouring, but the sky cleared up just in time for our departure. We sailed out to the bay, and according to Jeremy's wishes, we scattered his ashes. Everyone stood on the starboard side and threw flower petals out to sea. They swirled afloat as we said good-bye to him in our hearts.

After the motorcycle accident in Bermuda, Jeremy didn't swim because he was not supposed to get his left ear wet. He used to draw himself swimming in the ocean with many colorful fish. Now he is under the sea and free to go anywhere in the world.

Jeremy and I met twenty years ago completely by chance. I'm eternally grateful to him for having stopped by to buy that fountain pen in 1998. What incredibly interesting years we have shared since then! We kept taking on many challenges every day. The two of us knew how to have fun together no matter what.

Sometimes he would abruptly say, "If we weren't married yet, I would marry you again."

I would always reply the way both of us knew I would: "But we already are."

When my time comes and we see each other next, we'll get married again. I look forward to that. Till then, Jeremy.

Epilogue

JEREMY'S GALLERY AND CAFÉ

On September 22, 2017, the day before what would have been his seventy-fifth birthday, I opened Jeremy's Gallery and Café to hold his last art show for him and thank his fans and friends. The space was situated on the second floor of a ferroconcrete building in Motomachi, Yokohama. Jeremy and I used to take a walk and shop there. It was about sixty square meters, in the center of which was Jeremy's eight-feet-long drawing table. It usually had fourteen seats for visitors to sit down and have a cup of coffee while viewing Jeremy's works of art hanging on the walls. For the two years the place was in business, I served his favorite coffee, Colombia Supremo, and his favorite sweets. I held seven jazz flute matinees (twenty-six people maximum in the audience), two video shows respectively entitled "JEREMY STEIG, Everyday Life" and "Jeremy Plays in America," and a reading session of the *Flute Fever* liner notes.

Running this gallery and café was quite rewarding for me. I met so many people from different parts of Japan who thanked me for the opportunity to find out more about Jeremy or own one of his drawings. True, I set the place up, but it was the music Jeremy had played throughout his life that motivated people to come. The place was proof that he had touched many people by doing what he loved to do, and that means he had a nice life.

Some customers told me that they had heard only *What's New*. But they repeatedly came, talked with me or other customers about whatever they wanted to talk about, had a cup of coffee, looked closely at the works on the wall, and gradually opened up to the complex world of Jeremy Steig. Young people who have just started to listen to jazz or are lovers of music from the '70s came out of curiosity and became more interested in the times they have missed.

On top of the couple of stacked up wooden boxes used as bookshelves, below a framed photo of Jeremy on the wall was a notebook in which customers put down their thoughts or a message to Jeremy. Initially, I intended to obtain contact information on customers so I could invite them to the jazz flute matinees and other events, but everyone wrote such emotional messages to both of us. One man wrote that Jeremy had saved his life (with his music, I presume). Another wrote that he had listened to his records hundreds of times since high school. They all had personal memories about Jeremy and how they had come to know his music and art.

About a year after opening the place, I decided that I'd take the notebook to Jeremy as a souvenir. I now plan to be cremated with it.

ABOUT THE AUTHOR

Jeremy Steig (1942–2016) was an American jazz flutist, who is also known as a pioneer of jazz rock, or fusion. A gifted artist, he drew many of his LP covers, starting with his debut album *Flute Fever*. In addition to the regular concert flute, he played various flute-family instruments including piccolo, A-flat piccolo, alto flute, bass flute, and bass flute in F. He also recorded himself playing glass and plastic bottles percussively.